Decentralized Finance (DeFi)

How to Trade, Borrow, Lend, Save, Invest in Cryptocurrency Peer-to-Peer (P2P) Yield Farming, and Investing for Beginners

Naoya Yoshikawa

Introduction

Decentralized finance, or DeFi, is a means for making financial commodities available to the general public over a decentralized blockchain network. As a result, rather than going via intermediaries like brokerages or banks, it is open to anybody. In addition, unlike a bank or brokerage account, DeFi does not require a Social Security number, government-issued ID, or proof of address. Instead, DeFi refers to a system in which sellers, buyers, lenders, and borrowers connect peer to peer or with a strictly software-based intermediary rather than a firm or organization conducting a transaction using software developed on blockchains.

To achieve the goal of decentralization, various protocols and technologies are employed. A decentralized system, for instance, might be made up of blockchain, open-source technologies, and proprietary software. Smart contracts make these financial products possible, which automate agreement terms between sellers and buyers or borrowers and lenders.

DeFi solutions are intended to eliminate intermediaries between transacting parties, regardless of the technology or platform used.

Although the amount of money and trading tokens trapped in smart contracts in its ecosystem has been constantly increasing, DeFi is still a young industry with a nascent infrastructure. As a result, DeFi is subject to little or no regulation or control.

Decentralized finance, or DeFi, intends to eliminate intermediaries between parties in a financial transaction by utilizing technology.

DeFi consists of stable coins, a software stack, and use cases that allow for app development.

DeFi's use cases and infrastructure are still being developed.

What Exactly Is DeFi?

The use of technology in financial services isn't new. Nowadays, technology is used to complete most banks and other financial services organizations. However, technology's role is limited to a facilitator in such transactions. Companies must navigate the legalese of several jurisdictions, competing for financial markets and differing standards to complete a transaction. DeFi, with its stack of standard public blockchains and software protocols on which to build them, puts technology at the forefront of financial transactions.

DeFi is associated with blockchain and cryptocurrencies. However, it has a far broader scope. Therefore, it's vital to understand the existing condition of the finance ecosystem to comprehend the thought processes that resulted to the development of decentralized finance.

Modern financial infrastructure is built on a "hub and spoke" model. London and New York, for example, serve as operational hubs for the financial services industry, influencing economic activity in spokes— financial powerhouses or regional centers such as Milan or Mumbai, which may not be as globally important as hubs still serve as nerve centers for their respective economies.

Economic hardship or prosperity radiates outward from hubs to spokes and the rest of the global economy. This interdependency paradigm is repeated in the functioning of global financial services corporations. They have headquarters in hubs across the world and local branches, partnerships, and investments. Because of the size and scope of their operations, they are subject to a phalanx of laws and regulations in each of their financial jurisdictions. Their reach has made such institutions systematically critical to the global economy's stability and must maintain or build new financial services infrastructure.

Though this model functioned successfully in the previous century, the financial crisis and, subsequently, the Great Recession exposed its inadequacy. A domino effect of tumbling economies and the commencement of the global recession resulted from the balance sheet difficulties of a few significant banking institutions.

Decentralized finance makes use of technology to disintermediate centralized models and allow anybody, regardless of age, ethnicity, or cultural identity, to access financial services from anywhere. DeFi services and apps are generally based on public blockchains, and they either replicate existing products built on common technical standards or offer novel services tailored to the DeFi ecosystem. DeFi applications, on the other hand, give consumers more control over their money through personal wallets and trading platforms that cater to individuals rather than institutions.

Decentralized Finance is DeFi

Decentralized finance, or DeFi, was coined in a Telegram conversation in 2018. That's when a group of software engineers and entrepreneurs struggled to develop a name for their movement of automated, blockchain-based financial services capable of displacing traditional banks.

DeFi has increased in popularity over the last three years. A crypto wallet allows a user to exchange digital assets, obtain loans, and purchase insurance, among other things. More than 10 million users have downloaded Meta Mask, one of the most popular digital wallets used to access these networks, which has almost $90 billion in collateral.

The foundations of decentralized finance can be traced back to the 2008 bitcoin whitepaper, which laid out the groundwork for a unique virtual money system; a few years later, Ethereum was born. In her book The Infinite Machine, Camila Russo, creator of the crypto news service The Defiant, writes, "Bitcoin wanted to be peer-to-peer money." "Etherum wanted to be peer-to-peer everything."

DeFi is a combination of encryption, finance, and software development, and it has its jargon and lexicon. So let's break it down.

What is DeFi?

DECENTRALIZATION

Decentralized finance is defined by the fact that it is decentralized. For instance, bitcoin: The original crypto asset is essentially a decentralized ledger (the blockchain), with transactions stored in databases on many distinct computers. Cryptography is utilized to secure that one record (which is scattered over numerous databases), and the computers keep track of each other to verify it hasn't been tampered with.

Bitcoin's decentralization is part of what makes it so difficult to destroy. It's nearly impossible for anyone to go rogue and change the virtual coin's rules because no single entity is in charge. Similarly, even if a government attempts to prevent a group of computers from supporting bitcoin, the digital asset may continue to function because other computers on the network preserve a comprehensive record of transactions and continue to run the show.

This notion is taken a step further with DeFi. Blockchains, such as the Ethereum network, which Canadian-Russian programmer Vitalik Buterin suggested in 2013, are used in decentralized exchanges and lending systems. Unlike the bitcoin blockchain, which was established to log bitcoin transactions, Ethereum's blockchain was meant to host applications. Consider Ethereum as a decentralized computer for which software developers may create decentralized apps (dApps). Ethereum's processing power is compensated in ether, which is presently the second-most valued crypto currency behind bitcoin.

The Ethereum network, like bitcoin, is difficult to shut down or corrupt.

GOVERNANCE

DeFi companies' decision-making, or governance, is frequently decentralized, from the fees they charge users to the products they supply. (Think of DeFi as direct democracy if the US political system is representative democracy.) A decentralized program may be driven by a single person or a small number of individuals at first. Still, as the project gathers traction, they frequently seek to step back and transfer it to the community that uses it. This transition might take the shape of a decentralized autonomous organization (DAO), which has its rules and regulations written in computer code and may issue governance tokens, which allow currency holders a say in decisions.

PEER-TO-PEER

The ability for two users to conduct digital payments directly to each other was one of bitcoin's fundamental advances. Of course, this is quite easy to do using metal or paper money in the physical world. However, before bitcoin, the only method to do so electronically was through a bank or a payment service like PayPal.

Going via these third parties creates a digital trace that may be tracked, and those firms might be "censored" by the government, meaning they could be forced to block transactions for political or other reasons. Bitcoin was created as a digital form of currency for peer-to-peer payments to circumvent this.

DeFi apps can also be peer-to-peer. For example, an order is processed via several intermediaries in a standard stock-trading transaction, including a broker and an exchange. At the same time, the shares are kept at a custody bank, which is responsible for preventing the securities from being lost or stolen.

A DeFi exchange (DEX), on the other hand, does not have such middlemen. For example, suppose you trade crypto tokens on Uniswap, a decentralized exchange based on the Ethereum network. In that case, those assets will wind up in your crypto wallet thanks to Uniswap's automatic programs known as smart contracts. As a result, fewer parties will take a percentage of your transaction.

NFTs and ICOs

Since its inception 13 years ago, blockchain has permitted a succession of digital gold rushes. Two of them are nonfungible tokens (NFTs) and initial coin offerings (ICOs):

INITIAL COIN OFFERINGS (ICOS)

ICOs are a type of crowdfunding, and they are frequently used to raise fund for open-source software initiatives.

ICO investors receive a unique token in return for their money, which may or may not grant them access to the software's unique features... or nothing at all.

ICOs can sound a lot like a stock offering—too much like a stock offering for the US Securities and Exchange Commission; coin offerings may not have the guardrails like auditing and disclosure that an initial public offering would be expected to provide in the regulated stock market.

According to CB Insights, ICOs raised more than $7 billion in 2018 before plummeting by over 95% to $371 million in 2019, the most recent year for which data is available, as regulators cracked down.

NONFUNGIBLE TOKENS (NFTS)

NFTs are similar to limited-edition trading cards, but they're only available online. Blockchain enables people to create unique digital goods such as art and collectibles, just as it enables users to establish ownership of their bitcoin holdings. One of the most well-known NFT sales was a collage by Beeple (also known as Mike Winkelmann), who sold it for $69 million at a Christie's auction. Unlike MP3s, which can be copied and pasted indefinitely, NFTs are intended to be unique and only have one owner at a time.

ICOs provided businesses and software developers with a method to acquire money without the support of an investment bank or the backing of a venture capital company, according to Matthew Leising, author of Out of the Ether.

Similarly, NFTs can provide a new revenue stream for musicians and visual artists. "NFTs are fascinating because they've demonstrated that a digital item can be scarce," adds Leising.

What Are the Components of DeFi?

DeFi's components are comparable to those of existing financial ecosystems in that they require stable currencies and a varied variety of use cases. DeFi components include stable coins and services such as crypto exchanges and lending services. Because smart contracts encapsulate the conditions and behaviors necessary for these services to exist, they offer the architecture for DeFi apps to run. A customized code, for example, is included in a smart contract code that describes the exact terms and conditions of a specific loan. Collateral may be liquidated if certain conditions or circumstances are not satisfied. TRather than a bank or other business doing it manually, this is done through a code.

A software stack contains all of the components of a decentralized finance system. Each layer's components are intended to perform a specific function in the creation of a DeFi system. Composability is a defining property of the stack because the components from each tier may be merged to build a DeFi program.

The DeFi stack is made up of 4 levels, as shown below:

Settlement Layer (also known as Layer 0): The settlement layer serves as the foundation for all subsequent DeFi transactions.

It is made up of a digital money or cryptocurrency and a public blockchain. This money is used to settle transactions on DeFi applications, and it may or may not be exchanged on public markets. The settlement layer includes Ethereum and its native token ether (ETH), which is exchanged on crypto exchanges. Tokenized forms of assets, such as the United States dollar, or tokens that are digital representations of real-world assets, can be used at the settlement layer. For example, a real estate token may represent the ownership of a plot of land.

Protocol Layer: Software protocols are pre-determined standards and guidelines that govern certain processes or activities. Similar to real-world organizations, this would be a set of principles and practices that all players in a certain industry have agreed to follow as a condition of operating in that sector. DeFi protocols are interoperable, which implies that many organizations can use them to build a service or app at the same time. The protocol layer provides liquidity to the DeFi. Synthetix, a derivatives trading platform built on Ethereum, is an example of a DeFi protocol. It is employed in the creation of digital replicas of real-world items.

Application Layer: The application layer is where consumer-facing programs are kept. In these apps, the underlying protocols are abstracted into simple consumer-focused services. Most of the bitcoin ecosystem's apps, such as lending services and decentralized cryptocurrency exchanges are housed under this layer.

Aggregation Layer: Aggregators integrate numerous apps from the previous layer to give a service to investors in the aggregation layer. For instance, they might make it possible to transfer money seamlessly between different financial instruments to maximize profits. Such trading actions would require a lot of documentation and coordination in a physical setup. On the other hand, a technology-based structure should smooth the investment rails, letting traders swiftly switch between different providers. Borrowing and lending is an example of a service on the aggregation layer. Cryptocurrency wallets and banking services are other examples.

The Current State of DeFi

The development of decentralized finance is still in its infancy. As of March 2021, DeFi contracts have a total value of more than $41 billion. Here, the total value locked is computed by multiplying the amount of tokens in the protocol by their value in USD. Though the overall amount for DeFi may sound substantial, it's crucial to realize that it's only an estimate because many DeFi coins lack adequate volume and liquidity to trade on cryptocurrency exchanges.

Infrastructural mishaps and hacks continues to plague the DeFi ecosystem. Scams also abound in the fast-evolving DeFi infrastructure. DeFi "rug pulls," in which funds are drained from a protocol and investors are unable to trade, are prevalent, however there are well-established procedures that can considerably lessen the risk.

The dispersed and open nature of the decentralized finance ecosystem may cause issues with present financial regulation. The current laws are founded on the concept of distinct financial jurisdictions, each with its own set of laws and norms. The decentralized nature of DeFi's transactions raises serious regulatory issues. For instance, who is culpable for a financial crime that occurs across protocols, borders, and DeFi applications?

Smart contract is another area of concern for DeFi regulation. Apart from Bitcoin's success, DeFi is the best example of the "code is law" idea, according to which law is a collection of rules created and enforced by immutable code. The smart contract algorithm is pre-programmed with the essential constructions and terms of service to conduct transactions between two parties. However, software systems might malfunction due to various factors.

What if a system crashes due to the erroneous input? Or if a compiler (the program that compiles and runs code) makes a mistake. Who bears responsibility for the changes? These and many more questions must be answered before DeFi becomes a popular system.

Advantages and disadvantages of DeFi

The strength of DeFi can also be its weakness:
Decentralization makes DeFi harder to censor or eradicate, but it needs a lot of processing power. Maintaining a database and records over a network of numerous machines slows down transactions and can increase transaction costs. The most popular blockchain for DeFi apps is Ethereum; the massive quantity of processing is currently pushing up costs and slowing down the network. However, other chains like Solana and Avalanche are gaining traction as Ethereum developers strive to figure out how to make it more scalable. "It's very

difficult to get performance out of blockchains," says Emin Gün Sirer, a Cornell University computer scientist and Avalanche adviser.

DeFi eliminates middlemen such as custody banks responsible for keeping assets (typically digital tokens) secure. That means you won't have to worry about a financial institution going bankrupt and taking your tokens with it or about the government seizing and confiscating your tokens. On the other hand, you and your passcode are the only ones who can keep your assets safe. If you lose (or someone steals) that passcode, all of your valuables are lost forever.

The DeFi upstarts frequently claim to be open to everybody. Without typical financial credentials like identity or a credit score, you might be able to secure a loan or trade virtual coins. That liberty has the potential to bring financial services to sections of the world that haven't previously had them or where they are too expensive or vulnerable to fraud or confiscation. However, the drawback is obvious: If no one keeps track of who uses a service or where they are, criminals might use the systems or run counter to regulations. The regulatory crackdown has already begun.

Although blockchains have proved difficult to crack, the smart contracts and apps that operate on top of them are only as smart as the individuals who created them. The code is usually open-source, which means it's available for everyone to examine and modify, making it more vulnerable to hackers. Much more programming code is audited for bugs and vulnerabilities these days. An increasing number of people understand the importance of formal verification (a process that uses algorithms to analyze other algorithms for flaws). However, according to Cornell's Sirer, a lot of money is still going into code that hasn't been shored up in that way.

Three dApps you should know about

UNISWAP

Hayden Adams, a mechanical engineer from New York, founded Uniswap, a decentralized exchange (DEX). The concept came from Ethereum co-founder Buterin's blog articles about creating an automated market maker and decentralized exchange. According to CoinGecko, a crypto-data website, Uniswap now enables $1 billion or more in daily crypto trade, and its governance tokens, UNI, have a market value of roughly $12 billion. Stani Kulechov, a law student, established AAVE in 2017. (originally called ETHLend). The platform enables users to lend and borrow crypto tokens; according to Defi Pulse, users have put up nearly $14 billion in collateral for loans on the network.

MAKERDAO

MakerDAO is a lending and borrowing platform based on the Dai stablecoin, pegged to the US dollar. MakerDAO was formed in 2014, with Rune Christensen as a co-founder. MakerDao claims to be one of the largest decentralized apps on the Ethereum blockchain and the first DeFi application to gain widespread popularity on its website. Users have put up around $6 billion in collateral on the system.

DeFi Process

From the way the term DeFi was defined in the very first section, you have a short idea about what it means, i.e. peer-to-peer network without any hindrance of the authorities. But how does DeFi work in our world? It has happened many times; a concept sounds successful and worthy in the textbook but in reality, it is dull and does not make any sense. However, DeFi has been in use for quite some time on the Ethereum platform and it has been popular among the users. Here are some of the key points that will help you understand the process of decentralized finance:

Eliminates intermediaries—The process of DeFi completely knocks out the intermediaries from the financial system. Many people view intermediaries (usually regulatory authorities that watch your every move) as a form of security. In the case of a centralized financial system, banks or financial institutions that have been powered by the authority of the Central Bank act as intermediaries. The financial institution ensures that all your transactions are safe and secure, as a result, your money flows through them before it reaches the second party. The result is that at the end of the day, these intermediaries have more power over you because they hold your money, and without them, the financial system will cripple. Decentralized Finance completely eliminates these intermediaries or third parties from the financial system.

Uses Smart Contract feature—After eliminating the intermediaries in the system, you will need someone who will record your transaction and keep an account of your funds. The DeFi system uses the smart contract feature on the Ethereum platform that acts as an account. This account will then hold all your funds and use them for transaction as per the given set of instructions that you have enclosed in the smart contract. By leveraging the smart contract and the cryptocurrencies, DeFi makes every transaction smooth and possible without any involvement of a third party or a middle man.

Gives back control—The problem with the centralized system is that the control lies in only one hand and that is the regulator. This enables them to exploit their authority and sometimes overlook the flaws in the system. DeFi has decentralized this control by establishing a peer-to peer network that involves transactions between two parties. It means that you are in control of your funds and transactions without any authoritative hassle. DeFi has made decentralized financial systems a reality, which would have only been a dream a few decades ago.

Accessible to everyone—There are people around the globe, situated in certain geographies, who cannot avail any banking services, which serves as a limitation for them to open a bank account. In a traditional financial world, anyone without a bank account is restricted from doing any transaction as a bank account verifies your identity and serves as a proof for all the transactions. In the world of DeFi, however, one does not necessarily face the same level of restrictions. Currently, even those people who do not have any access to banking or financial institutions will be able to enter into the new financial system through the decentralized finance system. Finally, they will be allowed to gain access to global methods of value exchange.

Characteristics of Decentralized Finance System

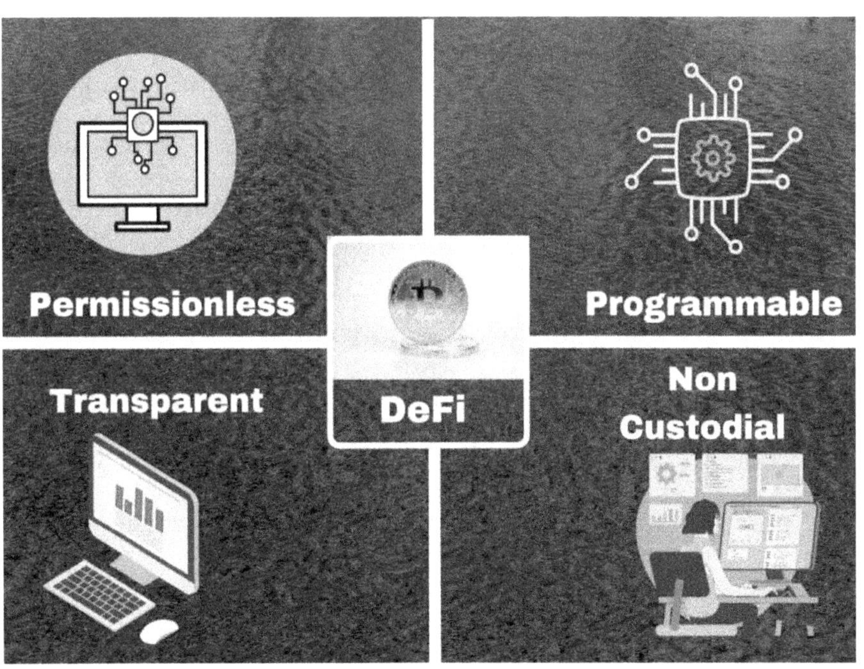

Since we have already discussed the meaning and the process of DeFi, you have a brief idea about the decentralized financial system. But as a beginner, you are still unaware about many things related to the decentralized financial system. In order to help you understand the term better, we will be listing down some of the main characteristics of DeFi to help you that will give you a quick insight before we move onto the greater details.

Non-custodial in Nature

Custody also refers to the control that you will maintain over the ownership of your assets. In traditional finance, the custodial ownership will remain with the intermediaries since they have a tight control over the financial transactions that involve your assets. The DeFi system follows a noncustodial approach whereby the owners maintain a control over the ownership of their assets without any third party involvement. For example, if you deposit your money into the bank account, your bank also possesses complete control over your funds, which they often use for lending purposes. With DeFi, you are still allowed to store your money in the form of crypto tokens in the safe wallets while maintaining control over those funds.

Open Source Technology

DeFi allows the users to build a financial system on a decentralized public network, which is powered by the blockchain technology that can be used by everyone. It is like an upgraded version of the internet whereby information can be sent to anyone around the globe in a matter of seconds. However, in the case of DeFi, you will be transferring the ownership of assets in the same way. If anything, it makes it more convenient for the users to transfer their funds through a digital network with ease compared to the traditional paperwork involving intermediaries. The best thing about open source technology is that anyone can access these platforms and reap the rewards of seamless and uncontrolled transfers of value (money).

Provides Transparency

DeFi is well-known for providing transparency to its users that is seldom neglected in a centralized system. Making the blockchain technology available to the public also ensures that all the transactions are verified by miners who solve complex mathematical codes and reap rewards in the form of crypto tokens. The transparency feature allows the users to avail information on every activity that is conducted on the blockchain network. This makes DeFi a legitimate and a transparent financial system as against the centralized network.

Composability

When you hear someone saying that the "system is composable," it simply means that it is designed using various parts that can operate together to provide the best service to its users. In a technological sense, the parts can operate together by communicating with each other through different codes. DeFi is a composable system that is essentially like a lego, whereby different applications are constantly interacting with each other without any permission. These applications keep communicating with each other and they leverage every code and utility in the system to provide the best user interface to its audience.

Fully Decentralized Network

The operations under the DeFi system are fully automated by the blockchain technology, which means that there is no need for a third person intervention. Traditional finance not only consists of third parties (financial institutions and regulators) but can also be a hassle with tons of paperwork and restrictions. DeFi is a paperless, technological, decentralized system that gives back the power to its community rather than controlling their every action and placing restrictions on their every move.

Secured Network

Most people are highly concerned about security when it comes to digital assets. It is easy for the attackers to infiltrate the system and steal the tokens. There have been instances where many people have lost their crypto token because the attackers hijack their wallet, leaving them penniless. However, you can build a DeFi system that is immune to the online threats from cyber attacks and hackers. The smart contract mechanism ensures that the system verifies your transaction while maintaining the data integrity so that information can be smoothly passed on across the system. Transmitting the data through a secured network that is established by the blockchain technology, DeFi could establish a safe financial network that can verify all the transactions.

Looking at all the key features of DeFi it is safe to say that it could be one-of-kind technology that could forever revolutionize our financial system.

Decentralized Finance and Open Finance

In order to establish the difference between these two concepts, it is important to understand the term "open finance." We all know decentralized finance, or DeFi, allows peer-to-peer connection that eliminates the intermediaries from the financial system. However, our world is still under the centralized monarchy. Central Banks are still the regulators of the financial system, so the decentralization of control remains a distant dream. Open finance is a concept that capitalizes on our current financial system and makes it much more effective.

Understanding the Term "Open Finance"

Hearing the term "open finance" might make you think that it is a service that is available to all. As I have already mentioned, open finance is yet another upgraded version of our centralized system. This means that all the banking services and financial intermediaries will still exist in your system. The only thing that differentiates open finance from traditional finance is the involvement of technology. Traditionally, people would go to the banks, handle the paperwork, and then get a loan or even have an account open.

Open finance has only made things easier as they have adapted technology into their overall process. What open finance does is use application programming interfaces, or APIs, that run on a code, which is used to communicate information among the different platforms. This will sound a bit similar to what I had spoken previously about DeFi explaining the composability feature. However, instead of a peer-to-peer network here, the information is usually shared among the intermediaries themselves, so from one bank to another. Although, open finance brings the ease of working using the technology with itself, it does not necessarily eliminate the centralized system.

DeFi, on the other hand, is a completely new and seamless way to handle your financial transactions. Using DeFi, we can open up the financial services to the public by increasing the chances of financial inclusion of various classes of people, reducing the extra costs and also eliminating the intermediaries. Hence, open finance may seem a bit similar to DeFi in the sense of operations, but the control will still remain centralized.

Why Is Open Finance Flawed?

Open finance has proved to be an excellent solution that has thumped out traditional banking systems. As per an article written by Vince H in 2021, the open banking system has been growing at a remarkable pace in the UK. After getting launched in 2018, the open banking system has created a vast base with over three million users, more than 300 providers regulated by the law, and over six billion API calls that are addressed every year. From the statistics itself, it is clear that open finance has been raging since its inception. The pandemic crisis only accelerated the adoption of open finance in the banking and financial system.

Although open finance has a much greater scope compared to traditional financial systems, it isn't exactly the solution. Open finance, theoretically speaking, should be beneficial to all forms of customers and even include those who are unable to access the centralized system. The reality is that, because open finance is just another top up version of our centralized system, it does not necessarily change anything. People are still availing the banking services through open finance but through technological means, whereas those who have limited access remain in that space.

If this continues in the future, open finance will not have much space to grow. In its own way, open finance is still better than our previous financial system, but it is flawed. This is exactly why DeFi could be a better solution, as it is a completely autonomous system with a similar technological adoption and fully decentralized, giving access to everyone, irrespective of their limitations.

Why Is DeFi the Future?

DeFi didn't exactly have a very easy start. Earlier, people were still wary of an unregulated financial system that could potentially change their lives. The centralized financial system has crippled us to an extent where we might question the safety of any system that seems to challenge it. However, DeFi was slowly adopted and, more now than ever, it has been the need of the hour.

Since its launch, there have been many decentralized apps, and some of them include decentralized exchanges such as Uniswap. What makes these exchanges different from our stock exchanges is that they will not hold back the funds to restrict you from executing the trades. DeFi also makes it possible for you to take on loans without going through all of the paperwork. For example, Compound is like a P2P lending platform where you can borrow money against a collateral or even earn interest against it. DeFi has been scaling and growing continuously. According to an article written by Natalie Zhang for CNBC in September 2021, it is that DeFi assets in the crypto market have increased from $4 billion in 2018 to $93 billion as of June 2021.

Looking at all the key characteristics that I have listed in this chapter, it can be anyone's guess that DeFi is much more robust and a reliable mechanism compared to the previous financial system. Imagine having complete control over your actions so that you can do what you want and change your life. DeFi is doing the same thing, except, in this case, you will have a better hold over your finances and data. Blockchain technology is supreme and most definitely the future of the financial system.

Based on what we have seen in this chapter, now you have a better idea on what DeFi means and the various features of the DeFi ecosystem.

Defi Lending And Borrowing Platforms

Decentralized Finance (DeFi) aspires to fill the void left by traditional banking. As a result, it has become one of the most popular movements to emerge from the crypto markets. It now functions as a new financial service enabler, meeting the conditions for broad adoption of Blockchain and cryptocurrencies.

Some of the most significant advancements in the bitcoin business have occurred due to the increase in DeFi lending platforms. As a result, it is the fastest growing industry and has steadily increased for several years.

Its rise to prominence began in the summer of 2020 when the prices of several DeFi platform tokens skyrocketed. There are many top DeFi lending platforms to select from, but do your homework before settling on one.

Top 15 DeFi Lending Platforms (2021)

DeFi Lending and Borrowing

DeFi lending services, like traditional peer–to–peer lending platforms, allow users to lend their assets to others. They receive interest payments in exchange. Because these platforms mostly trade in cryptocurrencies, they exclusively get cryptocurrency interest payments. DeFi platforms function without the use of middlemen; the financial gains are paid directly to the users.

The benefit of this platform is that anyone may take out a loan without going through any KYC or AML checks, and they also don't have to reveal their identity to a third party. This increases the accessibility of financial services.

DeFi services are more secure than centralized lending platforms because of the use of Blockchain.

You must provide collateral worth more than the loan value because DeFi platforms are anonymous.

Why Decentralized lending?

The leading Ethereum DeFi platforms have given a whole new meaning to the term "finance." It provides lenders with a variety of loan options and benefits. The following are some of the benefits of decentralized lending:

Hedge Funding- The crypto market is so diverse that it sends most investors packing. As a result, if you don't want to get burnt in the market and want to avoid price volatility, DeFi gives you the option to keep crypto for a certain period. It also allows traders to invest crypto for cash to meet other needs without having to sell it.

Earn interest by retaining crypto assets- You don't have to sell your crypto assets to avoid the bears; instead, you can lend them out at good interest rates that are specified in a contract. You earn money plus the interest within the specified time.

Less paperwork- Unlike traditional centralized banking, DeFi systems do not need a lot of paperwork. It's a simple process that just a few clicks on a Decentralized application.

How does DeFi Lending work?

Decentralized lending is as simple as lending money to someone by placing your hand in your pocket. However, the smart contract and decentralized program represent your mediators and negotiators. Let's see an example: if you want to give a $30000 loan using DApp, all you have to do is click a few buttons, and you're done.

Because you must choose any DApp application that gives a smart contract and borrowers, the entire process is extremely quick and uncomplicated. You must choose the loan's interest rate, enter it into the app, and the loan will be approved. Once you've found the borrower, the smart contract would automate both the loan and borrowing arrangement.

Best DeFi lending platforms

Selecting the right platform is essential as a borrower or a lender. Always consider the important elements, such as interest rates, and check whether they contain the assets you want to borrow or lend, as well as the level of safety and security.

Here is a list of the best DeFi loan platforms, compiled after extensive study, from which you may select one that best suits your needs:

BEST DEFI LENDING PLATFORMS

Whether you're a borrower or a lender, selecting the right platform is important. Always consider the important elements, such as interest rates, and check whether they contain the assets you want to borrow or lend, as well as the level of safety and security.

Here is a list of the best DeFi loan platforms, compiled after extensive study, from which you may select one that best suits your needs:

1) Aave

It's a non-custodial, decentralized, open-source liquidity market protocol in which you may participate as both a lender and a borrower. It is based on Ethereum and allows users to borrow money through a simple and user friendly interface. In addition, it renders a dual DeFi token model, i.e., LEND and a Token.

The a Token model is an ERC-20 token in which lenders' interest compounds. At the same time, LEND is a governance token in which you can receive various loans and lending services like uncollateralized loans, Flash loans, rate switching, and more.

2) Maker

It's a decentralized borrowing and lending platform quickly becoming one of the greatest DeFi lending systems available. Maker is also known as the MCD (Multi-Collateral DAI) system. It has over $7 billion tokens locked in smart contracts.

MKR and DAI are the Maker's major assets, and both are ERC-20 tokens.

Once the smart contracts are in place, DAI is linked to the dollar for lending and borrowing.

DAO is an Ethereum-based decentralized lending service that supports the DAI, a stable token tied to the US dollar. It also allows users with access to ETH and Meta Mask to lend in the structure of DAI.

3) Uniswap

It's one of the most popular decentralized exchanges built on the Ethereum platform. It allows users to exchange between ETH and ERC-20 tokens on the-chair or earn a fee by giving any amount of liquidity; consequently, token swaps are done through liquidity pools. The good news is that there are presently no restrictions on Uniswap.

ERC20 tokens are exchanged using a simple user interface secure, undamaged, and non-custodial. On this platform, you can trade any ERC20 token or earn a fee by providing liquidity to the process. You can either add liquidity to an existing pool or create a new one.

Every liquidity pair is represented by an ERC20 token that is unique and easily transferable. So, setting up a liquidity pool on Uniswap is simple; all you need is a token pair for markets. Then, the market makers set the exchange rates who use the standard product market maker mechanism.

4) Compound

Borrowers and lenders can use this decentralized money market technology to secure their crypto assets into the contract. It is built on the Ethereum blockchain, allowing holders of digital assets to borrow and lend crypto in exchange for security.

It differs from other DeFi lending services in that it uses cookies to keep tokenization assets locked in their system. Additionally, users can add assets to their liquidity pool and earn compound interest.

Compound allows consumers to take out over-collateralized loans and manage several assets, in addition to being thoroughly reviewed and formally verified. It puts aside 10% of interest payments as reserves, with the remainder to liquidity suppliers.

5) InstaDApp

It's a secure smart wallet for decentralized financial transactions. The good news is that it is a multi-purpose platform that effectively handles digital assets. InstaDApp allows users to optimize, manage, and position assets to maximize profits across various protocols.

You can use this platform to get various services, including borrowing, lending, leveraging, swapping, and more. It's similar to a bank in that it allows you to combine services to meet your needs. In addition, it offers users a user interface to manage their DeFi investments and migrate to cheaper loan platforms with lower interest rates, such as Compound, Maker, and others.

They also provide you with a DeFi protocol smart wallet portal. The most appealing aspect of InstaDApp is that it is completely free to use; all you need is enough ETH to cover the transaction cost.

6) dYdX

It's an Ethereum-based non-custodial trading platform aimed at seasoned investors. It introduced margin trading, derivates, and options to the blockchain, ubiquitous in currency markets and traditional investments.

dYdX is a platform for lending, trading, and borrowing DAI, ETH, and USDC. It also allows users to trade cross margin and isolated margin utilizing a perpetual market contract of BTC/USDC with 10x leverage. The good news is that, unlike other DeFi lending platforms, it does not have a native token and instead charges trading fees in the supported coins.

They provide loans with a 125 percent collateral requirement and a 115 percent self-liquidation requirement. dYdX trades more than $35 million each day, making it one of the world's largest decentralized exchanges for crypto assets and derivates.

7) SushiSwap

Ethereum-based software aims to encourage a network of users to manage a marketplace where users can buy and sell crypto assets. It is extremely similar to UniSwap, except for the open-source code.

It also achieves its objectives through a series of liquidity pools. You can also create your liquidity pool by offering any combination of ETH and ERC20 tokens, as well as swapping one token for another. Users must lock up their assets in smart contracts, and traders trade cryptocurrencies from those pools; thus, the user experience is quite simple.

SushiSwap is unusual in that it allows users to exchange cryptocurrencies without requiring the services of a central operator administrator. Therefore, the decisions associated with it are made by holders of its native cryptocurrency.

8) Dharma Protocol

It's decentralized debt tokenization and financial application based on the Ethereum blockchain. Borrowers, moneylenders, and other fund managers can trade and share information here. It's a feature of decentralized finance solutions that aims to make financial services more accessible to the general public.

It comprises a Dharma Settlement contract, which is modeled after traditional financial instruments and stakeholders. Four major agents run this network: borrowers, relayers, lenders, and underwriters.

Simple operators are both borrowers and lenders, relayers are agents who assist borrowers in locating creditors to repay their debts, and underwriters are agents who detect the risk of default and shape the debt issue's conditions.

9) Curve Finance

It's a decentralized exchange and liquidity pool based on Ethereum that allows for efficient stable currency sales. It allows users to trade with little slippage, consistent coin swaps, and a low-fee algorithm. Curve Finance also creates revenue for liquidity providers by providing liquidity to other protocols such as Compound.

This protocol's liquidity is distributed over seven curve pools: Compound, BUSD, Y, REN, PAX, sUSD, and sBTC. Each pool issues its ERC20 tokens to liquidity providers, which may be traded for various distinct assets.

10) Balancer

It's an Ethereum-based automated market maker that allows you to acquire a token at the best price and swap it immediately. To make a fee from trading, you can also create personalized liquidity pools or add existing pools.

It differs from other decentralized lending platforms in that their liquidity pool consists of only two assets, whereas Balancers' pool consists of eight digital assets for improved liquidity. Another notable feature is that it allows any amount of tokens in a pool to have any weight.

The pool's design is entirely up to the developer, and it can be tailored to their specifications. There are many types of pools: private pools are for private use only and can only add liquidity from the pool's owner.

Pool owners have no particular privileges with shared pools, and anybody can add liquidity to them. The charge and weights are specified in here, and they are permanent.

Smart pools are similar to private pools, except that smart contracts control them. Anyone can add liquidity here as well.

11) bZx

It's a decentralized Ethereum-based platform for DeFi lending, margin, and leverage trading. bZx is a fantastic replacement for dYdX. It sets itself apart by offering a token system based on smart contracts. Users can utilize tokenized loans and tokenized positions to trade and lend crypto assets.

It differs from other DeFi platforms in that the relayers match the orders of lenders and borrowers so that borrowers can get margin loans. iTokens, pTokens, and BZRX tokens are the three major ERC20 tokens in their system. The first two tokens are used for lending and borrowing, whereas BZRX is used for governance.

They charge lenders a ten percent fee on their revenues, which they aggregate into funds to ensure that lenders are protected and covered even if the borrowers default on the loan.

12) Fulcrum

It's built on the bZx base protocol that supports Kyber Network Token (KNC), Ether (ETH), Chainlink (LINK), Wrapped Bitcoin (WBTC), and Tether USD. It is one of the most straightforward and effective lend and margin trade strategies.

Lenders and borrowers put orders through a relayer, and the borrower receives the margin loan after the order is matched with the lender. Because it does not employ a centralized pricing fee, it is a trustless margin platform. The good news is that it is rent-free and permission-free, so you won't have to pay anything.

They also include an off-chain "bounty hunter" tool that monitors the solvency of each margin account; if they detect a possibility of borrowed funds being lost, they commence position liquidation and return to the lender.

13) Yearn.Finance

It's a decentralized ecosystem aggregating lending platforms like Compound, Aave, and DyDx. They provide lending aggregation, Ethereumbased insurance, and yield generation.

This system is administered by a 9-member multi-signature wallet, which requires a majority of members to agree on any proposed modifications, with votes recorded on-chain. As a result, to be implemented, modifications must be signed by at least 6 out of 9 wallet signatures.

They ensure that end-users obtain the best interest rates by optimizing the interest accrual process. You can also deposit assets and convert them into tokens via this platform. It rebalances your liquidity provider automatically so that you earn the most return by substituting liquidity with the most advantageous lending service.

14) Synthetix

It is an Ethereum-based decentralized investing platform known as Havven, a stable coin project. It allows users to build and use synthetic assets, sometimes known as "Synths," which provide on-chain access to tokenized, synthetic representations of physical assets.

These synthetic assets mimic the value of real-world assets and allow crypto holders to trade non-crypto assets on a decentralized currency-based market using their funds. It also has its native token, known as SNX. Users can lock the collateral in ETH or SNX to mint the synths. The good news is that synths are ERC20 tokens that can be traded freely.

Synthetix allows users to trade over 30 synths that reflect a various commodities, gold, dollars, stocks, bitcoin, and indices, to expand the platform's existing derivate offerings. Trades are also conducted on the noncustodial platform but on a peer-to-peer basis.

15) CREAM Finance

Individuals and institutions can use it to get financial services because it is a decentralized lending platform. You must deposit an amount of cryptocurrency worth greater than the amount of cryptocurrency you'll be borrowing in USD to borrow funds through Cream Finance.

Cream Finance is a permissionless, open-source, and Blockchain independent protocol that supports Binance Smart Chain, Ethereum, and Fantom. It recognizes the proper borrowers utilizing proprietary technical solutions and makes money available only a few clicks.

It is a loan platform based on compound finance. This implies that the cream financing protocol is based on source code from various DeFi lending systems, such as UniSwap, Balancer, and others.

Decentralized Exchanges

DEXs are peer-to-peer markets where cryptocurrency traders can transact without entrusting their assets to an intermediary or custodian. These transactions are made possible via smart contracts, self-executing agreements written in code.

DEXs were intended to eliminate the need for any authority to supervise and allow trades within a given exchange. Peer-to-peer cryptocurrency trading is possible on decentralized exchanges. Peer-to-peer refers to a cryptocurrency marketplace that connects sellers buyers. They are often non-custodial, meaning that users retain control over their wallet's private keys. Users may access their cryptocurrencies via a private key, a sort of sophisticated encryption. After login into the DEX with their private key, users may immediately see their crypto balances. They will not be forced to provide personal information such as names or addresses, which is ideal for those who value their privacy.

Automated market makers and other innovations that handled liquidity related difficulties helped lure users to the decentralized finance (DeFi) area and contributed significantly to its growth. By optimizing token prices, slippage, and swap fees, while providing a better rate for consumers, DEX aggregators and wallet extensions fostered the expansion of decentralized platforms.

<u>What are decentralized exchanges?</u>

Decentralized exchanges use smart contracts to allow traders to execute orders without a middleman. On the other hand, centralized exchanges are run by a centralized institution, such as a bank, which is otherwise engaged in financial services and aiming to earn a profit.

Centralized exchanges account for the great majority of trading volume in the cryptocurrency industry because they are regulated businesses that store users' assets and provide easy-to-use platforms for newcomers. Some centralized exchanges also provide deposit asset insurance.

The services supplied by a centralized exchange are equivalent to those provided by a bank. The bank protects its customers' accounts and provides security and monitoring services that individuals cannot provide on their own, making money transfers easier.

Decentralized exchanges, on the other hand, allow users to trade directly from their wallets using the trading platform's smart contracts. Traders are accountable for their money and are liable if they lose them due to errors like losing their private keys or transmitting payments to the wrong locations.

Customers' deposited monies or assets are issued an "I owe you" (IOU) that may be freely sold on the network via decentralized exchange portals. A blockchain-based IOU is simply a token with the same value as the underlying asset.

Popular decentralized exchanges have been created on top of popular smart contract-supporting blockchains. They're constructed on top of layer-one protocols, which means they're immediately on top of the blockchain. The Ethereum blockchain is used to power the most prominent DEXs.

How do DEXs work?

Every trade incurs a transaction cost in addition to the trading fee since decentralized exchanges are built on top of blockchain networks that allow smart contracts and where users maintain custody of their assets. To use DEXs, traders interact with contracts on the blockchain.

Types of decentralized exchanges

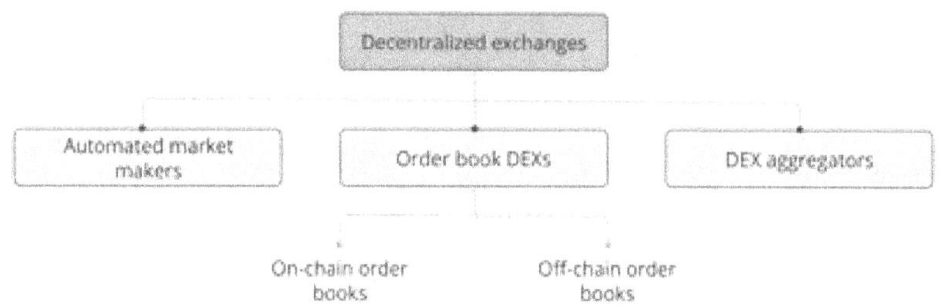

Automated market makers, Order books, DEXs, and DEX aggregators are the three basic forms of decentralized exchanges. All of them employ smart contracts to allow users to trade directly with one another. The initial decentralized exchanges employed order books similar to those used by centralized exchanges.

Automated market makers (AMMs)

An automated market maker (AMM) system based on smart contracts was developed to address liquidity. These exchanges were partially inspired by Ethereum co-founder Vitalik Buterin's article on decentralized exchanges, which described how to perform trades on the blockchain through token holding contracts.

These AMMs use blockchain oracles, which are blockchain-based services that supply information from exchanges and other platforms to establish traded asset prices. Instead of matching buy and sell orders, these decentralized exchanges' smart contracts employ liquidity pools, which are pre-funded pools of assets.

Other users finance the pools, and they are entitled to the transaction fees charged by the protocol for executing transactions on that pair. These liquidity providers must deposit an equivalent amount of each asset in the trading pair to earn income on their cryptocurrency holdings. If they try to deposit more of one asset than the other, the smart contract that runs the pool invalidates the transaction.

Traders can utilize liquidity pools to execute orders or earn interest without needing permission or trust. These exchanges are frequently evaluated according to the amount of

pool when one is more volatile than the other. cash locked in their smart contracts, known as total value locked (TVL) because the AMM approach has a drawback when there isn't enough liquidity: slippage

Slippage happens when a platform's lack of liquidity causes the buyer to pay above-market prices on their order, with larger orders facing greater slippage. Large orders are prone to slippage without deep liquidity. Hence a lack of liquidity might prevent rich traders from utilizing these platforms.

Impermanent loss, which is a direct outcome of depositing two assets for a certain trading pair, is another risk that liquidity providers face. Trades on the exchange might reduce the amount of one of these assets in the liquidity

If a highly volatile asset price increases while the quantity they hold falls, liquidity providers incur an impermanent loss. The loss is temporary since the asset's price can still rise, and trades on the exchange can bring the pair's ratio back into balance. The pair's ratio describes the proportion of each asset held in the liquidity pool. Fees gathered from trading can make up for the loss over time.

<u>Order book DEXs</u>

Order books keep track of all open orders and sell orders for specific asset pairs. Buy orders indicate a trader's readiness to bid for or buy an asset at a certain price, whilst sell orders indicate a trader's willingness to sell or ask for the item at a specific price. The spread between these numbers determines the depth of the order book and the market price on the exchange.

Order book DEXs have 2 types: off-chain order books and on-chain order books. DEXs using order books holds open order information on-chain, while users' funds stay in their wallets. Traders on these exchanges may be able to leverage their positions by borrowing funds from lenders on the platform. Leveraged trading raises a trade's earning potential while also increasing the risk of liquidation since it increases the size of the position with borrowed money that must be returned even if the traders lose their bet.

DEX platforms that keep their order books off the blockchain only settle trades on the blockchain to provide traders with the benefits of centralized exchanges. Exchanges can save time and money by using off-chain order books to make sure deals are performed at the prices consumers want.

Using off-chain order books helps exchanges increase speed and lessen costs. To ensure that trades are executed at the user's desires.

These exchanges also enable users to lend their funds to other traders to provide leveraged trading opportunities. Loaned funds accrue interest over time and are protected by the exchange's liquidation process, which ensures that lenders are compensated even if traders lose their bets.

It is vital to emphasize the importance of the order book. DEXs often suffer from liquidity issues. In addition, traders often adhere to centralized platforms since they effectively compete with centralized exchanges and pay extra expenses due to the fees needed to transact on-chain. While DEXs lower these costs, smart contract-related risks arise due to the need to deposit funds in them.

<u>DEX aggregators</u>

DEX aggregators employ various protocols and techniques to solve liquidity-related issues. These platforms effectively aggregate liquidity from several DEXs to reduce slippage on large orders, reduce swap fees and token prices, and provide traders with the best price in the shortest amount of time.

Other main goals of DEX aggregators include protecting consumers from the price effect and reducing the likelihood of failed transactions. Some DEX aggregators also leverage liquidity from centralized platforms to improve user experience while being non-custodial thanks to the use of certain centralized exchange integrations.

How To Use Decentralized Exchanges?

You do not need to sign up to use a decentralized exchange, and you do not even need an email address to connect with these services. Traders will instead need a wallet compatible with the exchange's network's smart contracts. DEXs' financial services are accessible to everyone with smartphones and internet connections.

Because each trade will involve a transaction charge, the first step in using DEXs is to pick which network a user wishes to use. The next step is to choose a wallet compatible with the chosen network and fund it with the network's native token. A native token is a token used to pay transaction fees on a particular network.

Wallet extensions that enable users to access their funds in their browsers make it easy to interact with decentralized apps (DApps). These are installed similarly to other extensions and need users to import a current wallet or create a new one using a seed phrase or private key. In addition, password protection is used to secure the system better.

Because they come with built-in browsers ready to engage with smart contract networks, these wallets may also include mobile applications so that traders may utilize DeFi protocols on the go. In addition, users can import wallets from one device to another to synchronize their wallets.

Following the selection of a wallet, it must be funded with the tokens. To pay for transaction fees on the chosen network. These tokens must be purchased on centralized exchanges and identified by their ticker symbol, such as ETH for Ethereum. After purchasing tokens, users must simply withdraw them to their control wallets.

It is important to avoid moving funds to the wrong network. As a result, users must transfer their funds to the appropriate account. Users who have a funded wallet can connect it through a pop-up window or by clicking the "Connect Wallet" button in one of the top corners of the DEX's webpage.

Benefits Of Using A Dex

Trading on decentralized exchanges may be costly, particularly if network transaction costs are high when the trades are made. However, there are some benefits to adopting DEX platforms.

<u>Token availability</u>

Before listing tokens, centralized exchange swill have to personally evaluate them and adhere to local regulations. Decentralized exchanges can include any token minted on the blockchain upon which they are built, implying that new projects will likely list on these exchanges before their centralized equivalents.

While this might mean traders can get in on projects as soon as possible, it also means that DEXs can be used to list all kinds of scams. For example, a "rug pull," or usual exit scam, is common. In addition, when the price of the tokens used to create liquidity on these exchanges rises, the team behind the project dumps them, making it hard for other traders to sell.

<u>Anonymity</u>

On DEXs, users' identity is protected when they swap one cryptocurrency for another. As a result, users do not require to go through a conventional identification process known as Know Your Customer, as they do on centralized exchanges (KYC). KYC standards require traders to provide personal information such as their complete legal name and a photo of a government-issued identity certificate. As a result, DEXs draw a considerable number of users who prefer to remain anonymous.

<u>Reduced security risks</u>

Because DEXs do not handle their assets, experienced bitcoin users who custody their funds are at a lower risk of being hacked. On the other hand, traders keep their cash safe and only interact with the exchange when they want to. As a result, only liquidity providers may be at risk if the platform gets compromised or hacked.

<u>Reduced counterparty risk</u>

When the other party in a transaction fails to meet their contractual duties and defaults on their portion of the bargain, this is known as counterparty risk. This risk is minimized since decentralized exchanges operate without middlemen and are based on smart contracts.

To guarantee there are no other risks while using a DEX, users can quickly run a web search to see if the exchange's smart contracts have been verified and make decisions based on other traders' experience.

Disadvantages Of Using Dexs

Despite the benefits listed above, decentralized exchanges have several disadvantages, including a lack of technical understanding required to interact with these exchanges, the number of smart contract vulnerabilities, and unvetted token listings.

<u>Certain knowledge is required</u>

DEXs can be accessed using crypto wallets that interact with smart contracts. Users must not only know how to utilize digital wallets, but they must also comprehend the security concepts involved in keeping their funds safe.

The relevant tokens for each network must be loaded into these wallets. Without a network native token, other funds may become stuck since the trader will not pay the fee required to move them. Therefore, you'll need certain knowledge to choose a wallet and fund it with the right tokens.

Furthermore, preventing slippage can be difficult even for experienced investors, if not impossible, when acquiring tokens with low liquidity. Slippage tolerance on DEX systems is frequently modified manually for orders. Additionally, regulating slippage is a technical process, and some people may not completely comprehend what it entails.

Traders who lack particular understanding might make a various mistakes that can result in a loss of funds. Withdrawing coins to the wrong network, incurring excessive transaction fees, and losing money due to temporary loss are just a few instances of what might go wrong.

<u>Smart contract vulnerabilities</u>

Smart contracts on blockchains such as Ethereum are open source, and anybody can review their code. Furthermore, smart contracts of large, decentralized exchanges are reviewed by reputable firms that help secure the code.

To err is human. Therefore, exploitable defects can still get through code reviews and audits. Auditors may even be unable to anticipate future vulnerabilities that might result in liquidity providers losing their tokens.

<u>Unvetted token listings</u>

Anybody can list a new token and combine it with other tokens to provide liquidity on a decentralized exchange. This makes investors vulnerable to frauds like rug pulls, that make them think they're buying a different token.

Some DEXs mitigate these risks by requiring users to check the smart contract of the tokens they want to purchase. While this technique is effective for experienced users, it reverts to specialized knowledge issues for others.

Traders can learn as much as they can about a token by reading its white paper, joining its community on social media, and checking for prospective audits on the project before making a purchase. In addition, this form of due diligence aids in the avoidance of frequent scams in which malicious actors exploit unsuspecting users.

<u>Decentralized exchanges keep evolving</u>

The first decentralized exchanges surfaced in 2014, but popularity grew as decentralized financial services based on blockchain gained traction. In addition, AMM technology helped alleviate the liquidity issues that DEXs had previously experienced.

Because there is no single organization authenticating information normally supplied to centralized platforms, it is difficult for these platforms to execute Know Your Customer and Anti-Money Laundering checks. Nevertheless, regulators may still try to impose these checks on decentralized systems.

Custodian regulations would not apply to these services since those that do allow user deposits still need users to sign blockchain messages to move funds off of their platforms.

Users may now borrow funds to leverage their positions, lend funds to earn interest passively, or supply liquidity to collect trading fees on decentralized exchanges.

More use cases may be generated in the future because these platforms are based on self-executing smart contracts. For example, flash loans, which are loans acquired and repaid in a single transaction, are an example of how decentralized finance innovation can create previously unimaginable products and services.

DeFi Opening Up Endless Possibilities

Until now, we have learnt everything about the DeFi system and even dove into the blockchain mechanics to understand how the entire process works. After going through all of the countless examples and processes, we have finally understood that DeFi is much more. It may have started out as some payment system that should be free from government control to change the map of the financial industry. Until now, we had only known how to use financial institutions, i.e. the intermediaries, to help us with our money management problems. However, when you look at DeFi, you realize that it has opened up all the doors that lead us towards our freedom. In this chapter, we will try to understand the scope of a decentralized financial system and also go through various examples of how businesses are adopting DeFi into their operations.

Scope of the Decentralized Financial System

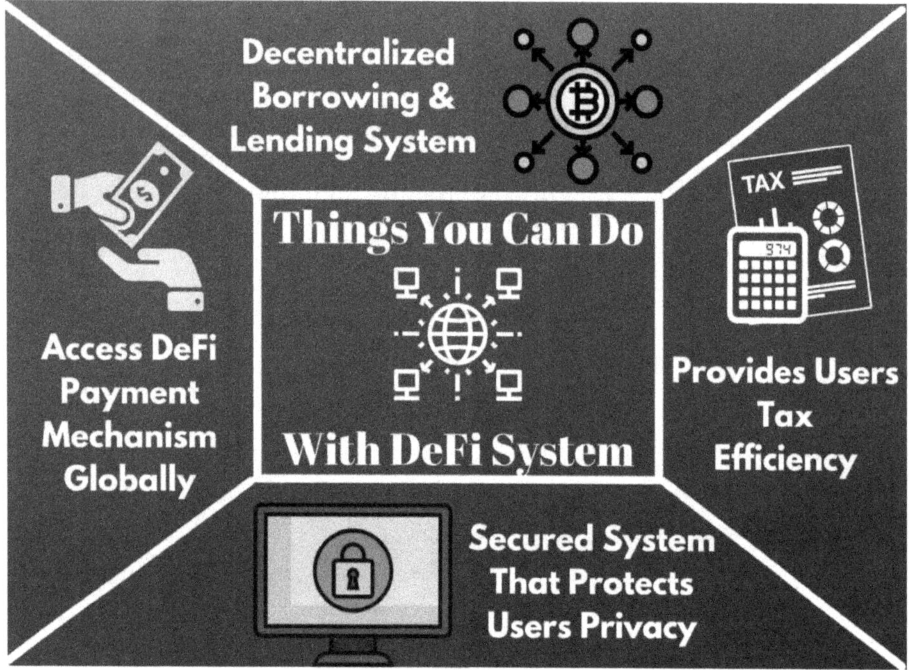

A decade ago, nobody would have imagined having a system that is fully automated and right under the owners control. DeFi has expanded the scope of our financial system and today, there is a decentralized alternative available for almost all the financial services. Not only this, but the Ethereum blockchain has also provided us with a base to create platforms and various financial products using its very own blockchain technology. Let us take a look at some of the endless possibilities in our financial system that have been powered up by Decentralized Finance:

<u>Quick Transfer of Money Across the Globe</u>

We had already seen that our traditional infrastructure is rather slow. In a fast-paced environment where everything can be done in a matter of a click, right from shopping online to sending a text, doesn't it seem weird that we still have to wait three to four hours for a wire transfer? The DeFi system easily solves this problem by simply creating a secured system powered by blockchain technology and peer-to-peer infrastructure that saves your time and energy.

If you take a look at cryptocurrencies, they were designed to send money across the globe in a secured way. Looking specifically at Ethereum blockchain technology, it uses the smart contract security over its network in addition to the cryptographic mining. With the help of cryptocurrencies such as Bitcoin and Ethereum, it has become easier to transfer your funds across the globe just like sending across an email. All you need to do is type in the user's address or an Ethereum Name Service (ENS) such as scott.eth or the user's account address from the wallet, and then the funds will be transferred to them in a matter of minutes.

<u>Streaming Money Globally</u>

Another choice that the whole DeFi system offers us is that we can stream our money across the globe using the Ethereum platform. For example, if you have to pay someone their salary which is due today, you can transfer the money and also give them access to their funds within seconds instead of waiting for two days. Not only can you make payments, but also rent something, like an electric car, using the DeFi system. In any case, if you don't wish to deal with Ether tokens because of volatility, you can simply opt for alternative currencies on Ethereum blockchain also known as stable coins.

<u>Decentralized Borrowing & Lending Protocol</u>

The traditional borrowing system is slow because it is still under the centralized regimen. Using decentralized borrowing mechanism is mainly distinguished into two categories:

Peer-to-Peer lending and borrowing, which ensures that the users can directly borrow funds from another user rather than going through the intermediary fuss.

Pool-based funding, which allows the lenders to provide their funds to a collective pool from where the borrows will draw our funds.

Decentralized borrowing and lending protocol may seem a bit risky considering the fact that users are lending their funds in a trustless system. What is the guarantee that your money will be repaid? To keep their users safe from any fraudulent activity, the platforms have developed a collateral system whereby you have to put the money you deposit into your account as a collateral before you proceed to borrow any additional funds. This way, the decentralized protocols ensure that the lenders get their money back and also allows the borrowers to get extra funds, which they can repay back with interest.

Let us take a look at some of the advantages of participating in a decentralized borrowing and lending protocol:

<u>Gives Users Privacy</u>

In the traditional system, the people have to share their personal details with the bank who needs to track them down on occasions where borrowers fail to repay the loans. Under DeFi, the users don't have to provide any identification to the other users. As it was previously mentioned, the borrowers have to put their deposit as a collateral, which the lenders will automatically receive if borrowers fail to repay the loan. Such a simple system allows you to borrow funds without undergoing the tedious credit checks or submitting the private data to the lenders.

Access Funds Globally

If the user can transfer money globally, they can also borrow money from a global pool of funds. The primary restriction with borrowing money from the banks is that it is restricted to your geography. Having access to the global funds allows the users to borrow more efficiently and also enjoy a suitable interest rate quote.

Factoring Tax Efficiency

Borrowing in a decentralized system will allow the users to easily access funds without having the need to sell their cryptocurrencies. As per the Internal Revenue Service, the gains on cryptocurrency are also capital gains, which is a taxable event. Under any circumstances, if the user has to sell their cryptocurrencies, they will be taxed for it. Instead of falling into the loop of the never-ending tax implications, DeFi allows the users to leave their cryptocurrencies as collateral and still acquire funds on their behalf. In short, people still get to keep their crypto tokens, acquire additional funds, and save themselves from the overall tax implications.

<u>Getting Access to Stable Currencies</u>

Cryptocurrencies have one common problem, which is the price volatility. The quick price swings don't make it easier for the general public and the financial industry to use such tokens. However, the DeFi community was able to solve this problem by introducing a new concept known as 'stable coins.' A stable coins value is pegged to an asset or, in our case, the US Dollar. The stable coin DAI that was introduced by MakerDAO usually fluctuates by a few cents, making it an efficient choice for a digital currency. The people from Latin America have used stable coins as a way of saving their money. It is safe to say the stable coins is much more successful and can be used as a daily currency.

<u>Start Crypto Savings</u>

Not only can you borrow funds through decentralized protocols, but also deposit the money and earn interest on it. Platforms like Compound Finance have made it relatively easier for the users to simply deposit any crypto asset into their account and earn equivalent interest rates on the same. The major benefit of crypto savings is that the interest rate the users earn through Compound is higher than the market rate that the banks will be offering to their customers.

Let us try to understand this concept with an example. The user decides to lend 100 DAI stable coins to a product called Aave. In return for lending their DAI, the user will receive 100 Aave DAI (aDAI), a token that highlights the user lending their money. The user will now start earning interest rate on their aDAI tokens and the balance in the wallet will keep on growing. The user can simply choose to withdraw the amount of their DAI tokens, which is equivalent to the amount of the aDAI tokens in their wallet at any point in time. When one can earn more interest through crypto savings, why would they pump all their money into the traditional banking system?

<u>Trading Crypto Tokens</u>

Ethereum has thousands of tokens on their platform that are getting mined every now and then. Through the decentralized exchanges (DEXs), you can simply exchange the ETH token for any other token. This is similar to the foreign exchange counters in different countries. The user isn't giving up any control over the asset they own, instead just exchanging it with another asset. The forex counters are bound to shut down at some point, but within the DeFi ecosystem, the DEXs are open and functioning 24/7 all year-round. Technological upgradation within the DeFi universe ensures that someone will be available to always accept the trade on the exchange.

Growing the Portfolio

The users can always grow their portfolio using various perks offered by the DeFi system. For instance, Ethereum offers the users certain fund management products that will enable them to build a portfolio with regard to their investment objective. The best part is that this protocol is automatic and open to all the available users without the involvement of a human manager who will not take any cut from the portfolio returns. For example, DeFi Pulse Index Fund was made to ensure that it automatically rebalances the user's portfolio by including all the top traded DeFi tokens based on their market cap. The user does not have to do anything except track their portfolio and they can simply withdraw the funds at any point of time.

Funding Ideas

There are many crowdfunding DApps, especially on the Ethereum blockchain, that allows three things to take place:

Since Ethereum blockchain is open for anyone around the globe, the crowd funders can take advantage of this feature and use the platform for raising funds.

DeFi is an open system that records all the transactions, so the users can track down how much money the fundraisers are raising while also tracing down the purpose for which these funds are being used.

Additionally, the fundraisers are also allowed to set up automatic refunds on the DeFi system if the minimum amount is not raised or the deadline isn't met.

Ethereum blockchain also uses a feature known as the Quadratic funding that ensures that projects with higher funding are also those that have unique features and better demands. For example, a matching pool of funds is donated by the users. After this, a round of public funding will begin whereby the users can sign their demands for a project by donating the funds. Once the funding round ends, the matching pool gets distributed to different projects. Unique demands are known for getting the highest amount from the matching pool.

The Initial Coin Offering (ICOs) has been one of the most famous crowdfunding demands all over the globe. Many investors have chipped in their funds on the pretext that the ideas will become successful in the future. Using the DeFi ecosystem, crowdfunding has become easier and efficient compared to the traditional way of raising the funds.

<u>Purchase Decentralized Insurance</u>

When DeFi was introduced, people believed that it was an illusion. When DEXs were launched, people thought trading cryptos was as good as creating a scam. Now that the entire financial system is built on DeFi, people are finally realizing it's potential. Until now, we have seen DeFi's potential that enables the user to invest in cryptos, start their own savings, borrow and lend funds, etc. It is time to introduce the concept of decentralized insurance, which aims to make insurance affordable and transparent while speeding up the entire process.

DeFi will automate the entire insurance industry, which will ensure that the coverage is reasonable for the users and the pay-outs are rapid compared to the slow system in the current times. However, Ethereum, which is known for building multiple DApps, also suffers from some bug glitches, so currently all the decentralized insurance products are focusing more on protecting their customers' funds. But there are many insurance projects that are trying to build coverages for any uncertain situation in our lives. For instance, Etherisc's crop cover is mainly aiming to help the smallholder farmers from Kenya against any type of drought or flooding. Now, the traditional insurance would be a costly business for such farmers, but with decentralized insurance, they can easily afford a cheap cover.

<u>Decentralized Portfolio Managers</u>

In the traditional system, keeping a track of the borrowed loans, personal investments, and stock trades is burdensome. The loans may be from another bank, the personal investments will be with some famous broker, and the stock trades will probably be with another broker who charges some cheap brokerage. In short, everything in the centralized system is a bit haywire, and keeping a track of each document will be bothersome. The DeFi system solves all of this problem by bringing everything under one roof. There are some DApps that allow the users to track all the activity from one place and the advanced interfaces also ensures that users can take advantage of the additional features of the platform.

Looking at all of the various possibilities of the DeFi ecosystem, it is understandable that decentralized finance is a better choice over the traditional counterpart. A decade ago, only crypto tokens were invented using the blockchain technology, which would be used for transactions. Today, our entire financial ecosystem can be easily powered by blockchain technology thanks to the concept of DeFi. Until now, we have only seen something that is the tip of the iceberg. Many things are yet to follow in the DeFi universe, which we will be able to witness and experience in the future. Since most of the scope has only been restricted at an individual level, let us now check out how DeFi is also getting adapted into businesses to help them operate effectively.

FinTech Startups Adopting DeFi Solutions

Not only has DeFi changed the functionality at an individual level, but also at a company level. In most cases, we have only discussed how DeFi is changing the personal finance landscape without touching upon the ecosystem that is actually responsible for helping in this change. There have been many startups and businesses who have slowly started exploring the DeFi option to either scale up their operations or help individuals adapt DeFi into their lives. Here are some of the most interesting DeFi startups that have come to life in the recent years:

DigiliraPAY—Blockchain Payment Gateway

By now, we all know that transactions through blockchain technology are faster, efficient, and transparent compared to the centralized banking system. To take advantage of this exact feature, Turkish startup DigiliraPAY decided to develop a decentralized payment gateway that is powered by the blockchain technology. Using the DigiliraPAY business, owners can receive payments in crypto tokens, but later they can cash them out in fiat money. Not only this, but users can also store money in the form of cryptocurrencies, which can be utilized while shopping or transferred to a friend without any additional commissions. DigiliraPAY also uses smart contract technology to ensure that all the transactions are secured.

TrustWorks—Financial Inclusion

People belonging to the marginalized section or those who can barely afford to spend their wages are usually the ones without a bank account. The centralized system has too many restrictions and barriers to entry, which prevents most of the people from even borrowing the funds or investing their money. To solve this problem, the DeFi ecosystem was developed so that everyone around the globe, irrespective of their geography or status, can avail basic financial services.

TrustWorks, a British startup, decided that they will help the underbanked section of the society by letting them avail the benefits of the decentralized financial system.

TrustWorks is powered by blockchain technology and uses stable coins to deliver fast-paced transactions to its users. Since this is a self-custodial solution, the users can also integrate it into their wallets where they store their money or take advantage of its features on their smartphones. Through the TrustWorks system, many mobile operators and humanitarian networks have been able to provide their users with low-cost yet effective financial services.

GoldFinX—Decentralized MicroFinance

Small and medium enterprises (SMEs), and some poor individuals in need of money go and borrow funds from informal lenders. The problem with these lenders is that they charge a higher rate of interest, which is more than what the banks would charge their customers. Those who can barely afford to churn their turnover or earn their wages will also find it difficult to repay the loans with higher interest rates. Thus begins the debt trap where all the poorer people get stuck because of an inefficient system. The DeFi ecosystem introduced the concept of decentralized microfinance solutions that lets the SMEs borrow funds at a lower interest charge. Not only this, but SMEs can easily lend their money as well and earn some interest on their borrowed funds.

A Singaporean startup, GoldFinX, decided to use the DeFi microfinance solutions and provide microfinance services, Artisanal Small Gold Mines (AGSM). This is to mainly support all the workers that earn low wages through such high-intensive labor work. GoldFinX also has its own token called GiX, which is being traded on decentralized as well as centralized exchange terminals. The value of this token is secured by the accumulation of gold, making it the most feasible option for the mine workers. More importantly, GoldFinX provides microloans to the AGSM, which helps them in adapting sustainable mining within the community.

These are just a few names that have flourished since the beginning of their journey into the DeFi universe. There are many other startups and businesses which are also adopting DeFi solutions or blockchain technology into their daily operations to run them efficiently and transparently. But, by now, you have heard the term blockchain too many times to even ignore it.

Blockchain Technology

The most important and primary component for DeFi to function is the blockchain technology. Blockchain serves as the fundamental base for all the cryptocurrencies, which are decentralized anyway, so DeFi is primarily powered by the blockchain technology.

What is Blockchain Technology?

In the simplest terms, blockchain technology is a distributed ledger that works on a decentralized framework that will keep a record of every transaction and track down all the business assets. Let us understand this through an example: Person A decides to lend some money to Person B and both of them have a mutual agreement that B will repay all the money by the end of two months with a two percent interest rate.

Now, all of this agreement is word of mouth, there is no written evidence as such claiming B has to repay the funds back to A. By the end of two months, A is still waiting for B to pay back the funds. The catch here is that B claims that they never borrowed any funds from A and the lack of physical evidence anyway proves to be an unfavorable situation for A. So, at the end of the day, B enjoyed betting in casinos using A's money while A was the sore loser.

Now let us understand this same concept using blockchain technology. Person A and B are two strangers. A wants to lend his money and earn some interest while B wants some urgent funds. Since both are needed by each other, the system allows B to borrow funds from A while locking in his deposit as a collateral. A also starts earning some interest for lending funds to B. The exchange that took place between A and B is all recorded in the system, which is transparent and secured. Blockchain technology simply ensures that all of the transactions take place smoothly, but also remain recorded so that the users cannot cheat the system.

Decentralization - Component of Blockchain Technology

Another feature of blockchain technology that always stands out is decentralization. This is the most important feature and the main reason why blockchain is used in the DeFi ecosystem. The decentralized system prevents any third party involvement, which means Person A need not go to a bank to deposit his money and Person B need not wait for days before they get the loan approval.

Everything is quicker than the traditional system mainly because it does not allow the participation of intermediaries. Now the only question that remains is if there is no third party to monitor the transactions, how will they be executed. Prior to recording the transaction in the distributed ledger, they need to be executed in the system. The DeFi system automates all the transactions using the smart contract feature on the platform.

Once these automated transactions are executed in the system, they will be recorded and the data is publicly available to all the users. Since blockchain technology also adapts a peer-to-peer mechanism (cuts off the intermediaries), it is building a trustless system among the users. Unlike the centralized system where you have to trust the banking authority, DeFi powered by blockchain technology enables you to control your money without trusting anybody in the system.

Smart Contracts: Automating the Transactions

The second most important component in the DeFi ecosystem is the smart contract feature. Smart contracts are like a program that are stored within the blockchain technology. This program will only run on the platform when certain conditions are met. However, within the DeFi system, a smart contract feature is usually used to automate the transactions. Using smart contracts, the platform will automatically execute all the transactions, such as transfer of funds from Person A to Person B. This smart contract feature was mainly imbibed into the system so that the users don't have to waste their time waiting for an intermediary to execute their transactions. Using this program is the best way to automate the workflow without causing any delays on the platform.

How Does a Smart Contract Work?

Smart contracts are known for following commands, which means that they will follow simple statements such as, "if….then," which are written in code language. Based on the conditions, the network of computers will only execute the actions if all of the listed conditions have been met. The following actions can be executed using the smart contract feature:

- Transferring funds to concerned parties
- Sending notifications to a user
- Issuing a ticket

For example, if you decide to transfer some funds based on some preconditions in the contract, the blockchain will get updated once the transaction is completed. Another important thing that one must remember is that the transaction cannot be changed since the smart contract has already been set up. The parties who have been granted permission will only be the ones who can be the result of these transactions.

Advantages of a Smart Contract

There are many benefits to the smart contract feature that has been adopted into the DeFi ecosystem. Some of them are as follows:

Speedy process—The smart contract process is simple; if the condition is met, the contract will get executed. There is no need to involve any third party or go through the tedious paperwork, which will cause delays and waste time. In addition to this, there is no chance for an error since the system is fully automated, which will rarely be the case with all the manual paperwork.

Transparent system—No third party involvement also means the information will rarely be altered by the middle person for their own personal benefit. Both the users will receive their encrypted copies of a transaction, which only highlights transparency in the entire system.

Secured network—The smart contracts are encrypted with a security code, which makes it hard to hack into the system. Even if the cyber attackers alter a single record in the distributed ledger, they may have to alter the entire chain since it is all interconnected with each other.

By now, we have understood the concept of blockchain, briefly followed by the smart contract program used in the DeFi system. However, there is a third component in DeFi that helps the ecosystem work autonomously from anywhere, and the major reason why DeFi has been growing all these years.

<u>Peer-to-Peer Lending Mechanism</u>

The first peer-to-peer technology on a decentralized network was established back in 1969 when Advanced Research Projects Agency Network (ARPANET) was found. ARPANET was the greatest predecessor to the P2P technology followed by famous platforms like Napster in 2005. However, despite being the most efficient system in the past, P2P was overshadowed by the centralized structure everywhere. But since we are on the subject of P2P technology, let us go back to the basics and understand what it means.

What are Peer-to-Peer Networks?

Within the peer-to-peer ecosystem, two or more computers are communicating with each other by sharing data or code without the approval of a central server. Every computer in the peer-to-peer networks will act as a data point within the large network and each of them will keep the copy of the same information that is shared across the network. On the other hand, the central server will connect all the miscellaneous client servers to a single repository. This is a primitive technology that is still being used by the centralized system. For instance, the stock exchange is the central server that receives all the data from the intermediary servers that are operated by the brokerages.

Even the traditional financial institutions, such as the banking system, operate on a centralized structure, which ensures that they have control over the customer's money. However, peer-to-peer technology adapted within the DeFi ecosystem is set to be a paradigm shift that will truly transform the way our financial system operates. DeFi has also gone a step ahead and introduced a peer-to-peer lending mechanism that allows its users to borrow funds directly from others without having the need to approach the intermediary. Due to its infrastructure, peer-to-peer lending is also known as social lending that has become a form of alternate finance, which has witnessed extensive growth over the years. Let us take a small glimpse at the basic comparison between traditional and crypto-based P2P lending.

Traditional vs Crypto-based Peer-to-Peer Lending

Traditional peer-to-peer lending has its funds denominated in fiat currency such as the US Dollar, and operated outside the conventional banking infrastructure. This form of lending is mainly used by the SMEs as an alternative source of funding since the tight banking regulations prevent them from accessing their loans. There are many companies, such as Lending Club, Prosper, Peerform, etc. which are competing in this space. However, traditional P2P lending still heavily relies on fiat currencies whose value deteriorates depending on the rate of inflation in the market. Overall, the traditional P2P lending mechanism is still risky and can collapse any moment if the global economy faces a financial meltdown.

On the other hand, crypto-based P2P lending uses decentralized infrastructure to curb the central authorities from gaining control over the market. The entire crypto-based P2P lending mechanism is powered by smart contracts, which automates the entire lending process, making it a time-saving proposition. Within the DeFi ecosystem, crypto P2P lending operates in such a way where the user has to deposit excess funds as collateral before they proceed to borrow additional money. In an event where the borrower fails to repay their borrowed funds, this collateral will automatically be transferred to the lender. Protocols like Compound allow their users to deposit funds within specific pools and earn interest by lending their funds. However, the entire crypto P2P Lending infrastructure is powered by smart contracts so the lender does not have to go hunting for his money since everything will automatically be executed on the platform.

The crypto-based P2P lending is proving to be a better option than people originally expected. A research study published by Shadaab Khan, Aarti Goswami, and Vineet Kumar on Allied Market Research in May 2020 highlighted that the global P2P lending market value stood at $67.93 billion. This market value has been forecasted to reach $558.91 billion, which will grow from 2020 to 2027 at a CAGR of 29.7%. Looking at the figures, it is an obvious guess that most of the P2P lending is bound to come in from the crypto-based decentralized assets in the future. By eliminating the intermediaries from the credit system, crypto P2P lending has allowed the users to have rapid settlement with lowered infrastructure costs.

Looking at all the three factors: blockchain technology, smart contracts, and peer-to-peer lending; they have completely redefined the financial ecosystem through revolutionizing technological adoption. Since we have the working knowledge of how the entire DeFi system functions, it is time to understand those people who are responsible for bringing this magic to life.

DeFi Developer

The pace at which the new DApps are getting discovered is astonishing. Developing every decentralized app is a time-consuming process. But along with having the right platform to establish a particular protocol, such as Ethereum, it is also important to have the right person with the desired skills to develop the DeFi projects. A DeFi developer has all the relevant knowledge with their amazing skill set, which can help the users build a protocol using blockchain technology. Let us take a look at some of the skills that the developers must possess to build a protocol.

<u>Skills Required to Become a DeFi Developer</u>

A DeFi developer, just like any other regular developer, should have a strong background in Computer Science and IT products. However, as a DeFi developer, one has to understand three major components of cryptocurrencies: cryptography, data structure, and networking. Along with the technical skills, DeFi developers should also have an understanding of the project that they have decided to take up. For instance, one need not necessarily have any knowledge of the financial structure to work on a crypto project, but possessing the right knowledge with the required skills can help them while they work on the project. It is always reasonable for the DeFi developers to understand the objective of the project and how it will add value to the users. But if we have to head into the specifics, there are two significant factors that DeFi developers must have a working knowledge about:

ERC-20 tokens—These tokens are available to all the Ethereum blockchain users as they have been developed extensively after they met a list of crypto community standards. ERC-20 tokens have been developed using smart contracts that automate the system using the programming language called Solidity.

Solidity—Solidity is a programming language that is used to power up smart contracts. This was developed through the influence of Python, C++, and Javascript programming languages. Solidity is extensively used on Ethereum blockchain since it was designed to run Ethereum Virtual Machine.

Ethereum blockchain and Solidity programming language is a good start for all the beginners who wish to become a DeFi developer. In addition to this, one can always showcase their skills by building their own DeFi projects.

<u>Job Opportunities for DeFi Developers</u>

The job market for DeFi developers is tight and competitive. To get qualified for the job, DeFi developers must ensure that they build their skills and reputation in the market. The best way to get a job as a DeFi developer is by crypto-based job platforms that will specifically offer you developer jobs. For example, platforms like Crypto Recruit Ethlance are assisting the budding developers in their journey by offering them recruitment through numerous job offers.

Additionally, you can also keep an eye on social media platforms such as LinkedIn, Twitter, or even Reddit where many companies as well as individuals are posting about jobs or requirements for their own startups. When it comes to doing individual projects, it is always better if DeFi developers understand the project and then prepare to work on it. But DeFi has tons of potential which is yet to be unlocked, so developers still have lots to learn and grow in this space.

Now that we have a working knowledge of all the concepts and the technical information related to DeFi, it is time to move on to interesting topics.

Risk Management Strategies For Defi

The cryptocurrency economy has been completely altered by decentralized financing (DeFi). As a result, traders are interested in this segment because it is both a viable infrastructure project in the crypto business and a way to benefit from volatile token fluctuations.

At the same time, this volatility comes with significant risk. So let's take a look at a couple DeFi market tactics that might help mitigate these risks.

In 2021, overall funds invested in DeFi protocols are expected to increase from $20.1 billion in January to more than $106 billion as of the time of writing this book. Furthermore, the average daily trading volume on decentralized exchanges (DEX), a key component of decentralized finance, increased by 100%. It surpassed $2 billion in Q1 2021, but stayed below $1 billion in Q4 2020.

Decentralized finance allows investors greater control over their money, thus investors have been drawn to it from the start. While decentralized finance began with loans and credit, it has now expanded to include at least five fully functional, linked segments: blockchain, loans and credit, decentralized exchanges (DEX), insurance, and decentralized derivative platforms.

Despite its relative stability, the DeFi sector is nevertheless a dangerous investment. The high volatility of numerous project tokens surely draws new investors. However, a high return also entails a high level of risk. In DeFi, there are several successful risk management strategies.

This reduces the chance of a single item losing a large amount of value in the portfolio. The market cap to total value locked (TVL) ratio may discover prospective tokens. Tokens with the lowest correlation of these values might be regarded cheap, implying that there is reason to believe these assets will "catch up" and rise in value.

Traders may thus stabilize their portfolios for the medium and long term by purchasing these cryptocurrencies.

Choose projects on other blockchains, such as Ethereum or Binance Smart Chain, to further diversify your risks. Another alternative is to use negatively correlated tokens, which means that if one token is particularly volatile in day trading, you should balance it with a more stable asset. For example, the Uniswap (UNI) and Zilliqa (ZIL) tokens are rather stable assets.

It's even better to diversify your portfolio by adding an insurance project, because the need for capital protection in the decentralized financial ecosystem is only going to expand. Nexos Mutual, Cover, Etherisc, and Opyn are some of the projects that offer DeFi insurance. If an unpleasant event occurs unexpectedly, having these tokens in your financial portfolio will allow you to considerably mitigate the impact.

STRATEGY 2: STAKING

With stake-able tokens, you can also reduce the risks of value loss. Certain DeFi projects' cryptocurrencies allow users to benefit just by keeping them. Users of the international cryptocurrency exchange CEX.IO, for example, may earn up to 16% yearly interest on their tokens. And when the price of the currency rises, so does the reward from staking. For example, if a trader buys $100 in ZIL at $0.20 per coin and earns a 16 percent staking interest, they will receive around 580 ZIL at the end of the year. If the price has risen from $0.20 to $0.40 during that period, the trader will receive $232 when they cash out. The profit increases to 132 percent instead of 20 percent when the coin's price increases.

You can invest in stable coins that enable staking, like as Dai, to safeguard your portfolio from large fluctuations. As a result, the passive income from your tokens may both boost your overall profit from investing in the DeFi sector and protect you from any losses if the market falls. Traders can also restrict their losses to the amount of their staking reward potential. Traders can simply terminate their positions as soon as the losses on their holdings approach the profit they would gain from staking.

STRATEGY 3: HEDGING

When traders purchase an asset on an exchange, they instantly establish an opposing position in the underlying derivative in the classic hedging format. Such derivatives could be options, futures, contracts for difference. So, if a trader buys UNI on the exchange, they would sell a contract for difference for the same amount to hedge the risk of the asset losing value. Finally, if the value of UNI rises, the losses on the contract for difference will be reimbursed by the rise in the value of the cryptocurrency. If the price of UNI falls instead, the difference will be offset by the CFD's opposite position.

Specialized platforms offer derivative trading, and CEX.IO Broker is one of them. You can use it to profit from price swings in cryptocurrencies without having to acquire them in person, as well as to hedge assets you own. A contract for difference allows traders to avoid the uncertainty, technical risks, and complexity associated with DeFi by participating indirectly. In addition, the platform uses automatic protection orders, such as stop-loss and take-profit, to manage risks.

CEX.IO has built a complete trading and capital management environment. It enables users to profit from DeFi market movements to the fullest extent possible and, if required, to employ measures to protect their capital properly.

Right away, users are presented with a full solution. First, there's portfolio diversification: there are a lot of DeFi currencies to invest in and trade. Second, staking, for example, provides a larger yield than the network's rewards: for example, ZIL staking pays 16 percent interest, whereas the network pays just 14.2 percent. Finally, at CEX.IO Broker, DeFi coins can be traded as derivatives.

CEX.IO Broker's versatility allows you to establish up to ten accounts as part of a single user account and test alternative tactics independently of one another. A demo account is available for people who have never worked with the cryptocurrency market before. Traders can go to a genuine account and start trading the currency pairings they choose if they are confident in their abilities.

CEX.IO Broker is a margin trading platform that allows you to start trading with less money than you would with spot trading. This allows you to leverage your trading capital to grow your trading capital.

How Defi Is Revolutionizing Industry

Individuals and organizations are already beginning to investigate decentralized finance due to the significant increase in cryptocurrency investments (DeFi). So let us look at this growing market.

As you already know, Decentralised Finance (DeFi) is based on the peer to-peer idea, which eliminates the need for middlemen. DeFi democratizes finance and substitutes conventional centralized institutions like banks, brokerages, and NBFCs by relying on peer-to-peer philosophy and self executing "smart contracts" on the blockchain network (Non-Banking Financial Companies).

DeFi is a blockchain-based smart contract platform that requires no human interaction. This decreases the likelihood of mistakes while also increasing efficiency.

A DeFi protocol makes use of smart contracts, which are computer programs that operate on the blockchain network. The source code for most DeFi projects is open to everyone in the world to see and audit. Users of the DeFi protocol may use their wallets to connect with these smart contracts and transfer cash, borrow, lend, or use any of the DeFi's services.

DeFi projects on the blockchain network offer quick and affordable access to finance, as well as efficient lending and borrowing, as well as decentralized crypto and synthetic stock markets. Some DeFi projects, such as Uniswap, have evolved into extremely efficient worldwide financial markets that cater to both people and institutions due to their decentralized character. DeFi also eliminates intermediaries, allowing for more efficient and low-cost financial services.

Anyone with an internet connection may observe, audit, and see all of DeFi's transactions because it runs on a blockchain network and is typically open-source. In addition, blockchain data is immutable, which cannot be modified once it is on the blockchain network. This results in a code-based, trustless financial system. One such example is a Decentralised Exchange (DEX).

DEX'S GROWING POPULARITY

Decentralized Finance (DeFi) has succeeded to bring about a significant transformation in the financial industry in recent years. As a result, transactions on DeFi and Decentralized Exchanges (DEXs) on the blockchain network have exploded in popularity, with disintermediation as the key idea.

DEXs can have deep liquidity by offering asset-specific liquidity pools instead of order books on centralized exchanges, thanks to a technique known as "Automated Market Makers" (AMM). Users can provide liquidity to these liquidity pools and earn significant passive incomes through trading fees.

Unlike centralized financial services like traditional banking, DeFi firms don't need intermediaries or custodians to perform crypto asset purchasing, selling, lending, and borrowing. Instead, DEX users can engage directly with the blockchain system to make transactions or get services. Users may keep their cryptocurrency ownership and have total control over their assets in their wallets, thanks to the DEX's non-custodial design. DeFi and DEXs utilize "smart contracts," self-regulating computer code that runs on a blockchain network.

The Ethereum blockchain network is used for most DeFi projects since it is the first to provide an infrastructure that allows developers to create such decentralized apps (DApps). However, other blockchain networks such as Solana, Cardano, Polkadot, and others are in development and are gradually making the DeFi field more competitive.

DEXs and DeFi projects are steadily becoming a profitable choice for SMEs and startups in the FinTech field throughout the world, despite their complexity and steep learning curve. DeFi and DEXs across the globe provide easier access to cheaper credit, easy lending and borrowing operations. They are transforming the face of traditional financial institutions, thanks to reduced entry hurdles compared to traditional finance.

EXTENDING TO THE INSURANCE INDUSTRY

The insurance business has been one of the most influential DeFi use cases. While the current insurance system is hampered by complex paperwork, audit systems, and bureaucratic claim procedures, smart contracts can make it far more efficient. Insurance coverage for cryptocurrency on the blockchain network is also available through DeFi startups such as Nexus Mutual, Opyn, and VouchForMe. Inflationary pressures and falling interest rates in fiat currencies have made it difficult for middle-class individuals throughout the world to save and invest. DeFi projects like Dharma, PoolTogether, and Argent have provided risk-free savings and investing alternatives with no-loss saving mechanisms.

Since it supersede traditional banking systems, borrowing and lending protocols have become one of DeFi's most important uses. Compound and PoolTogether are two DeFi projects that focus on the peer-to-peer (P2P) borrowing and lending sector. Transactions have become quicker thanks to distributed ledger technology (DLT), particularly in the case of cross-border payments, where the cost of transactions and delays generated bottlenecks for both senders and recipients. DLT has democratized banking by allowing anybody to take out loans and even lend fiat against cryptocurrency collateral. In addition, the DeFi ecosystem has allowed tokenization, which allows for the creation, issuance, and management of digital assets on a blockchain network. This has lead to the emergence of a new type of economy. For instance, digital assets are being tokenized in the form of NFTs to create, store, or trade value. With the rise in DeFi adoption, more DeFibased prediction services have emerged, allowing users to exchange value by predicting the result of future events.

REVOLUTIONIZING THE GAMING INDUSTRY

DeFi allows people to bet on world events using platforms like Augur.

DeFi technologies have also found a large market in games and eSports. Game developers may now use deFi tokens for in-app purchases and loot box features. By allowing players to exchange unique tokens and allowing developers to establish their ecosystems and economies, collectible and trading games have become popular blockchain genres.

The aforementioned benefits of utilizing DeFi account for its rapid rise in recent years, with a market valuation of $128 billion. While decentralized exchanges provide numerous ground-breaking benefits, they also come with certain drawbacks. Unlike traditional banking, DeFi investments are not subject to regulation or insurance. Other crypto assets are used to secure DeFi loans. However, in the event of a downturn, the value of these assets may plummet, and they may even be liquidated. In addition, centralized systems may be used to recover lost data and account information such as passwords. If the seed phrase is lost when trading on DEXs, the user information and hence the funds may be irreversibly lost. Therefore, users must first assess the apps they're considering to verify they're secure and well-tested, as with any investment decision.

To sum it up, while centralized systems continue to dominate market activity because to user-friendly interfaces, security, regulatory control, and insurance options, the rise of DeFi has made room for decentralized crypto exchange protocols. DeFi will have to improve its capabilities and become more robust in terms of security and scalability as more individuals enter the digital asset industry. This has already begun with the upgrade of the Ethereum network to Ethereum 2.0. DEX will very certainly make cryptocurrency trading more fair, private, and independent in the near future, hence speeding up the evolution of decentralized finance and its supporting systems. The most recent developments and trends in cryptocurrency investing appear to bode well for Decentralized Exchanges.

Indicators Every Defi Investor Should Know

It can be challenging to keep up with the avalanche of new ideas in the DeFi arena, expanding rapidly. Fundamental analysis evaluates whether a business is overpriced or undervalued for investors and traders to make more informed judgments about their investments.

Do you want to know how to calculate the "intrinsic" worth of DeFi assets? Then, continue reading to discover some of the most effective measures for doing so.

Decentralized Finance (DeFi) evolves at such a breakneck speed that keeping up, much alone evaluating new ideas in a timely manner, can be challenging. In addition, the lack of a consistent technique makes it much more difficult — there are several ways to assess and compare DeFi technologies.

But don't be worried. We will go through some of the most widely utilized indications that might be useful in DeFi. Because a large quantity of data is publicly available on-chain, any trader or investor may easily use these indicators. Spencer Noon's discussion encouraged us to compile a list of them on this page.

Locked Total Value (TVL)

Total Value Locked (TVL) is the total amount of cash locked within a DeFi protocol, as the name suggests. TVL may be considered all of the liquidity in a money market's liquidity pools. In the context of Uniswap, TVL refers to the amount of money put in the protocol by liquidity providers.

TVL is a good measure to determine the general level of interest in DeFi. In addition, TVL may be used to compare the "market share" of various DeFi protocols. This is particularly beneficial for investors seeking discounted DeFi projects.

It's also worth noting how multiple denominations may be used to measure TVL. The TVL locked in Ethereum projects, for example, is usually quantified in ETH or USD.

P/S ratio (price-to-sales ratio)

The Price-to-Sales Ratio (P/S Ratio) relates the price of a company's shares to its sales in a more traditional business. The stock's cheap or overpriced status is then determined using this ratio.

Because many DeFi protocols are already profitable, a comparable metric may also be used for them. How can you use it? You will need to divide the protocol's market capitalization by its revenue. The main premise is that the lower the ratio, the less valuable the technique is.

Remember that this isn't the only approach to figure out how much anything is valued. However, it can provide you with a rough estimate of how fairly the market values a project.

Token supply on exchanges

Another option is to monitor the supply of tokens on cryptocurrency exchanges. Sellers that wish to sell their tokens often do so on centralized exchanges (CEXs). Users on decentralized exchanges (DEXs) now have a growing number of options that don't need them to trust an intermediary. On the other hand, centralized venues tend to have significantly better liquidity. This is why it's essential to monitor token supply on CEXs.

Here's a simple token supply assumption. Sell pressure may be larger when there are many tokens on exchanges. Because whales and holders don't keep their money in their wallets, they may be looking to sell them.

With that said, things aren't so simple. For example, many traders will utilize their holdings as collateral for futures trading. As a result, submitting a large balance to exchange does not always imply that a significant sell-off is on the horizon. Nonetheless, this is something you should keep an eye on.

<u>Token balance changes on exchanges</u>

We already know that keeping track of token supply is useful. However, merely looking at the token balances might not be enough. Examining recent changes in such balances can also be beneficial. For example, large token balance changes on exchanges can typically indicate a rise in volatility.

Consider the polar opposite of the issue we just discussed concerning token balances. If large holdings are being removed from CEXs, it might imply that whales are accumulating the token. Why would they withdraw their wallets if they planned to sell soon? This is when keeping track of token movements comes in handy.

Unique address count

While it has its limits, an increase in the number of addresses owning a certain currency or token should indicate higher usage. On the surface, it appears like having more addresses means having more users and increasing adoption.

However, this is a gameable metric. It's easy to generate hundreds of addresses and distribute funds to them, giving the impression of broad use. You should compare unique address count to other aspects, just like any other metric in fundamental analysis.

Non-speculative usage

So you're interested in investing in an emoji-based token that promises high returns, but does it truly work? If the main aim is to increase value, it could earn the Charles Ponzi seal of approval, but it won't last long.

To determine the real worth, you must first understand what it is used for. In an ideal world, you'd count the amount of transactions that aren't carried out only for the sake of speculating. This can be tricky, but a good place to start is looking at transfers that do not take place on centralized or decentralized exchanges. The goal is to ensure that the token is being used.

<u>Inflation rate</u>

Wow, a limited-edition token! Isn't it an good sign?

Not necessarily. The rate of inflation is another significant measure to watch. Currently, a limited supply does not guarantee a limited supply in the future, especially if more tokens are being minted. However, Bitcoin has a continually decreasing inflation rate, which should potentially prevent the depreciation of existing units in the future.

That isn't to say that every system should strive for the same level of scarcity as Bitcoin. For example, inflation isn't inherently bad in and of itself, but too much of it might lower your slice of the pie. Because no defined proportion is regarded as "good" or "bad," it's important to consider the amount while considering other metrics.

If you are an experienced cryptocurrency trader, you'll notice that many of these indicators are also employed in fundamental research for "conventional" cryptocurrencies.

Markets are illogical, unpredictable, and prone to severe volatility, as they always been. But, above all, doing your research is vital to success.

Make Money With Cryptocurrency

So you're interested in Bitcoin and want to convert it to cash. You've certainly heard of folks who made millions of dollars by getting in early and selling for a high price. Perhaps you have friends that make a living from bitcoin mining.

Everyone enters the cryptocurrency market with the goal of making money, but not everyone is successful. Many people either quit up or lose money due to their lack of understanding of how to generate money using cryptocurrencies.

CTA

The crypto market is still in its early stages of growth. However, as the value of crypto-assets rises, more individuals enter the market. These newbies are always trying to figure out how to profit from cryptocurrencies.

The good news is that there are a lot of methods to profit from cryptocurrencies. Since 2011, the bitcoin business has seen a constant increase in developer engagement, social media activity, and the number of start-ups launched.

Can You Make Money With Cryptocurrency?

Yes, you can make money with cryptocurrency. However, because of the inherent volatility of crypto assets, most of them are high-risk, while some need subject skill or knowledge.

One of the methods to generate money using cryptocurrency is to trade cryptocurrencies. Despite the daily average volume of cryptocurrency trades being only 1 percent of the foreign exchange market, the crypto market is volatile. So, there is the possibility for short-term trading.

Even though the cryptocurrency business is still small, it has a lot of room to develop. Along with some of the more well-known cryptos, such as:

- Bitcoin
- Cardano
- Ethereum
- Tether
- VTHO
- ElonGate

- AMP

- Dogecoin

- Iota

- Safemoon

- Stellar

- Moonshot

- Polygon

- Shiba Anu

Similarly, there are many crypto-buying platforms, such as Binance, Robinhood, and Coinbase, giving you lots of alternatives when it comes to generating money with cryptocurrency.

Apart from the obvious trading method, there are quite a few methods to make legal money using cryptocurrency.

Strategies for Making Money with Crypto

Strategies for making money with crypto depends on 3 mechanisms:

To begin, you can invest or trade on a cryptocurrency exchange. You can do this without holding any cryptocurrency at all, similar to how you can invest in gold on the stock market.

Secondly, you can lend and stake coins to the system or other users using the currency you currently own.

Lastly, you can participate in the blockchain system by receiving or mining coin incentives for your efforts.

Here are six techniques for generating money with cryptocurrencies based on these three mechanisms:

Investing

Investing is a long-term strategy that entails buying and keeping crypto assets for a lengthy period of time. Crypto assets, in general, are well-suited to a buy-and-hold strategy. This is due to the fact that they are extremely volatile in the short term yet have tremendous long-term development potential. The investment technique demands the selection of more stable assets with a lengthy lifespan. For instance, Etherum and Bitcoin have a track record of long-term price growth and may thus be considered secure investments.

Investing

Trading is meant to take advantage of short-term opportunities, whereas investing is a long-term strategy focusing on buy-and-hold.

The cryptocurrency market has a high degree of volatility. As a result, asset prices may move significantly in the near term.

You should possess the necessary analytical and technical abilities to be a successful trader. To make correct predictions regarding price rises and falls, for example, you'll need to analyze market charts on the performance of the listed assets.

When trading, you can take a short or long position based on whether you predict an asset's price to rise or fall. This means that regardless of whether the cryptocurrency market is bullish or bearish, you can profit.

Lending and Staking

Staking is a cryptocurrency transaction verification mechanism. You hold coins when you stake, but you don't spend them. You keep the coins in a cryptocurrency wallet instead. Your coins are then used to validate transactions on a Proof of Stake network. Doing so, you will be rewarded. To put it another way, you're lending coins to the network. This permits the network's security and transaction verification to be maintained. As a result, you'll get a reward that's equivalent to the interest a bank would pay on a credit amount.

The Proof of Stake algorithm selects transaction validators based on the number of coins you've pledged to stake. So, it consumes far less energy than crypto mining and does not necessitate the purchase of expensive hardware.

You can lend coins to other investors in exchange for interest. Many platforms facilitate crypto lending.

Crypto Social Media

You'll be rewarded for generating and curating content on several blockchain-based social media networks. In addition, you are often awarded the platform's native coin.

Mining

Cryptocurrencies mining is a way to generate money using cryptocurrency as the early adopters did. Mining is still a vital part of the Proof of Work system. It is where the cryptocurrency value is generated.

If you mine a cryptocurrency, you get rewarded with new coins. However, you'll require technical know-how and initial investment in specialized hardware to mine.

Mining is a subset of running a master node. It necessitates knowledge and a large initial and ongoing investment.

Airdrops and Forks

Airdrops and free tokens are issued to raise awareness. For example, an exchange might do an airdrop to build a large user base for a project. You can get a free coin by participating in an airdrop, which you can use to buy items, trade with, or invest in.

A blockchain forks due to upgrades or changes in protocol that create new coins. If you have coins on the old chain, you'll receive free tokens on the new one. This implies that you received a free coin because you were in the right place at the right moment.

How Does Bitcoin Work?

After understanding the origins and the meaning behind Bitcoin, it is important to also understand how the entire Bitcoin process works. The entire process of Bitcoin largely works in three steps:

<u>Step 1—Blockchain Technology</u>

The blockchain used on the Bitcoin network is more like a public ledger, which is shared among the users. The entire decentralized network of Bitcoin completely relies on this ledger. All the transactions that have been confirmed will be visible on the ledger.

In addition to this, your wallet will also calculate the balance that you can spend on other transactions, which will pave the way for the most recent transactions to be verified and also confirm that they are owned by a particular user. For example, person X is sending T amount of Bitcoins to person Y who is then sending U amount of Bitcoins to person Z. After tallying all these transactions, everyone will know where each user stands. Since all of these transactions are recorded on a "distributed ledger" available to the public, it provides transparency to the users and ensures that none of them can fake a transaction or even reverse it at any point.

Without any involvement of central authority, anyone can access the network irrespective of their country, race, gender or even ethnicity, which opens up a wide range of prospects for the internet. In the future, it is even possible to have systems where an Uber has its own blockchain wallet. The passenger traveling in the vehicle would have to transfer cryptocurrency to the car, which would only move after the funds were received in the wallet.

<u>Step 2—Private Keys</u>

When a transaction takes place between two users, there is an exchange of value among the Bitcoin wallets that will be visible on the blockchain network. The Bitcoin wallets aren't exactly openly accessible to everyone. They are secured by something known as a private key (that is like a secret data) that is used to sign the transaction. Private key is like a stamp or a mathematical proof that the following transaction has been through an owner's wallet.

The cryptographic signature also prevents the fraudsters from taking ownership of the transaction or even altering them once they have been issued. After the transactions have been issued, they will be broadcast on the blockchain network so that they can be confirmed and verified by the miners. Usually verification of a single transaction takes upto 10 to 20 minutes after it undergoes the mining process.

Step 3—Mining Process

The Bitcoin mining process is also referred to as the "distributed consensus system" that is a generally used mechanism to confirm the pending transactions on the network. What mining does is it protects the network neutrality, imposes a chronological order on the blockchain, and authorizes various computers to agree with the system. Before confirming any transaction, they must be loaded into a block (a record that will confirm various waiting transactions) that should follow the cryptographic rules before getting verified through the network.

As we already discussed, this process will prevent anyone from modifying the transactions within the block. If any of the transactions is altered within the block, it will invalidate all other upcoming blocks. Beyond this, mining also ensures that individuals cannot add any new blocks easily to the blockchain network. This prevents the individuals from controlling what can be included or replaced in the blockchain network so that they can roll back on their own spending.

Blockchain miners are also rewarded for verifying each block containing numerous transactions. The reward undergoes an event known as halving, which usually cuts the reward into halves for mining every 210,000 blocks or every four years. This entire reward process is designed in such a way that the Bitcoin mining will continue upto 2140. Once all the Bitcoins are mined through the codes and all the halving process is complete, the miners will be incentivized through the fees that will be paid by the network users, which hopefully will remain on the lower side. The third halving process took place on May 11, 2020 and the reward for each block was quoted at 6.25 Bitcoins.

Although Bitcoin is the very first decentralized system that started back in 2009, there were many other systems and altcoins that have shown greater efficiency. For example, if you look at Ethereum, it has developed a platform that offers its users unique features that are much more than transferring funds. Since the launch of Ethereum, many other platforms have been launched which use the Ethereum blockchain. One such platform is MakerDAO, which we will discuss in the next section.

2017—MakerDao Was Built

We have all seen a payment system that has been decentralized without the needs for authority. However, our financial system isn't exactly restricted to the money transfer. The banking system's main business is to borrow and lend money as they earn incentives through an interest factor. Keeping this in mind, Rune Christensen decided to start MakerDAO, an organization that develops various technologies on the Ethereum blockchain, to allow its users to lend and borrow crypto tokens without the needs of an intermediary.

How Does It Work?

MakerDAO follows a simple protocol that allows anyone who owns Ether (ETH) tokens or a MetaMask wallet (a plugin that allows the users to easily access the Ethereum decentralized application, or DApps, smoothly) to lend themselves money using their very own stable coin DAI. The users can lock up a certain amount of their ETH tokens, which will serve as a collateral on MakerDAO's smart contract, allowing them to create the equivalent amount of DAI. If you lock up more ETH tokens, you will generate more DAI. Once you pay back the DAI loan along with the required fees, the ETH tokens will be automatically unlocked. But MakerDAO is simply the best example of a DeFi system in the real world.

Let us understand this using an example where the current price of Ethereum is at $150 and we decide to deposit 1 ETH token at that price. We decided that we will lend ourselves 50 DAI, which is collateralized at a rate of 300%.

Our position is bound to be safe as long as the Ethereum price remains above $75. The $75 is based on the calculation of 50 DAI*150% assumed Collateralized Debt Position (CDP). The ETH token will remain locked until one year after, which, when we repay the 50 DAI, it will automatically get unlocked. Once the position is closed (including paying off the CDP), we will have to pay an annual stability fee on Ethereum platform. As of June 21, 2021, MakerDAO has slashed their stability rates from 5.5% to 3.5% (Young, 2021).

What Is the Need for DAI Tokens?

We have so many cryptocurrencies, so why do we only need DAI, a perpetual stable coin for DeFi lending and borrowing mechanisms? Aren't all cryptocurrencies decentralized in their own way? First of all, DAI, as we all know, is a stable coin meaning the token value will remain fixed even if the Ethereum price keeps changing. Most of the cryptocurrencies are volatile in nature with huge price swings, which is a problem over a period.

DAI is not the first stable coin to be used for such a project as there have been multiple stable coins in the past going by the names of Tether and TrueUSD. The risk of dealing with such stable coins was that the custodial party that owns US Dollars will refuse to redeem these stable coins because of the regulatory risk. This brings us all back to square one where the centralized regime has overpowered us with authority.

There were two major problems with primitive stable coins concept:

It was never permissionless to begin with, so decentralization would have never worked on such currencies.

There is no such trustless system because we have to put our faith in the custodial system having to believe that they actually hold the US Dollars as against their intention of creating an artificial inflation.

Looking at both these issues, it is relatively obvious why the primitive stable coins were a failure. On the other hand, DAI is powered by the decentralized Ethereum blockchain, which has only led to its success among the users. But to take all of this one step ahead, a new marketplace was built, which went by the name of Compound Finance that will be discussed in the next section.

September 2018—Compound Finance Roared to Life

Compound Finance is like a money market place that allows its users to deposit the money and earn some interest on it, just like a savings account, or they can borrow funds against their funds. Compound crypto that is used on the platform exclusively is also built as a DApp using the blockchain technology. In short, the entire platform follows DeFi protocol that uses the smart contracts to store your data and manage the capital on the platform.

The best part about Compound Finance compared to other DeFi platforms is that it allows any user to easily connect with the platform, deposit their money, and start earning interest through a Web 3.0 wallet called MetaMask, which relies heavily on Machine Learning and Artificial Intelligence components. The feature of permissionless protocol ensures that anyone who owns a crypto wallet and a steady internet connection can easily interact with the platform.

How Does Compound Finance Work?

There are many crypto platforms that restrict the users to use their tokens only. Take for example MakerDAO, it only restricts itself to the Ether tokens. However, the Compound DApp supports numerous crypto assets such as Ether, DAI, Tether, USD Coin, Wrapped BTC, etc., and there are additional tokens which will be added in the future. If you own any of these crypto assets, you can easily engage in the borrowing and lending activity on the Compound platform. Compound Finance works using three different elements:

cTokens

The supplied assets on the Compound platform also known as the positions are tracked through tokens or, in case of Compound, they are called cTokens. These cTokens are ERC-20 tokens (Ethereum Request for Comment) that are usually the tokens issued on the Ethereum blockchain. ERC-20 tokens will represent a claim over a portion of the assets that you deposit on the Compound platform. For example, if we decide to deposit ETH on the platform, it will be converted into cETH or, if you deposit DAI, it will change to cDAI.

Interest Rates

If we supposedly deposit multiple crypto assets, then all of them will earn interest based on their fixed rate on the platform. In our case, cETH and cDAI will each earn their own interest rate that has been fixed on Compound. The interest earned via cTokens on the platform can also be converted to the value of an underlying asset that you are holding. However, in order to earn an interest on the Compound platform you must hold the ERC-20 token.

The interest rates are factored in by the demand and supply of the crypto assets in the market, which is the main reason why they keep fluctuating all the time. For instance, if there is a ton of money stored in our Compound wallet, chances are that the interest rates will be lower. Now you may ask why? Simply because the borrowers already have a lot of funds available to them so that will not provide the lenders any opportunity to add more funds to an already big pool.

The pool of money is dependent on the type of the cryptocurrency that you own. Suppose you have funds of a particular cryptocurrency that is small, the chances are the interest rate will be high. This is because there is a small pool of funds available for this currency and the lesser the funds in the pool, the higher the interest rate earnings on that pool. Another advantage of the Compound platform is that any user can borrow funds from the large pools and repay those same funds into the smaller pools. By doing so, the user is cutting down on their expenses and paying a lower interest rate.

<u>Borrowing & Lending</u>

To start the entire credit process on the platform, the users will have to first set up their MetaMask, which will open up the possibility of unlocking any asset that you can use while borrowing and lending. On Compound, the borrowing process can be complicated but it is definitely not the same as the time-consuming traditional system. Before borrowing the funds, you will have to deposit some cash as collateral on the platform. After depositing some money into the account, the users will earn some "Borrowing Power" which is a criteria used by the platform that allows the users to borrow. For example, every asset on Compound has a different level of borrowing power. Based on the user's borrowing power, they can borrow assets based on their required choice.

However, the lending process is very simple on the Compound platform. All that needs to be done is to unlock the assets that the user wants to provide on the platform to supply liquidity. After unlocking the asset, the user has to sign a transaction through their wallets post which they can start supplying their capital. The unlocked assets instantly become a part of the pool and they also start earning interest rates in real time. During this entire process, the supplied assets will be converted into cTokens, since that is the only way the platform functions.

Compound also has a concept of overcollaterization whereby the borrowers have to deposit funds that will exceed the value they will borrow from the platform. This is only done as a safety measure to avoid any form of liquidation on the platform.

What Makes Compound Finance Useful?

After looking at how the borrowing and lending activity is carried out in the Compound Finance world, it is safe to say that the system is far more efficient compared to our banking structure. Just imagine waiting for days or even weeks until you get an approval to borrow the loan from the bank. We have also discussed that the interest rate earned in savings accounts is very low. Compound offers you the opportunity to not only borrow funds through a direct protocol but also earn interest on the funds that you will be lending to the borrowers. There is no counterparty involved in this whole process as all the assets are simply held by the smart contracts, also known as liquidity pools.

What Is Compound Governance and How Does It Work?

Compound Finance's protocol has a governance system, which is slowly getting decentralized on the platform. The users can participate in this governance system by holding the right amount of COMP tokens. All the users on the platform receive COMP tokens that are generated every 15 minutes as the miners mine the Ethereum block. The number of tokens received will depend upon two factors:

Interest rate of every crypto asset that has been pre-decided on the platform.

Number of transactions that each user has participated in using the protocol.

Any user who owns one percent and above from the total supply of the COMP tokens gets to participate in the governance system. The main advantage of participating in the governance system is that the users are allowed to submit a proposal or vote on any of them since they suggest making any changes on the Compound blockchain network. In this case, one COMP token counts as one vote on the governance system.

Looking at the Compound Finance system, it is understandable that the platform is a bit more advanced than MakerDAO and also has potential to outperform in the longer run. But Compound wasn't the only thing where people stopped inventing new protocols using the Ethereum blockchain. To make this process interesting, a new player entered the ring whose background we will be discussing in the next section.

November 2018—Uniswap Came Into Existence

Uniswap is an Ethereum-based cryptocurrency exchange that is completely decentralized and operates on a new trading model, which is known as automated liquidity protocol. If one sees the common stock exchanges, it is a well-known fact that they are regulated by a central authority such as the Securities Exchange Commission (SEC). Uniswap was built back in 2018 using the Ethereum blockchain and it quickly became the second largest crypto project ranked by the market capitalization. Since Uniswap is popular among the users, it is highly compatible with all the ERC-20 tokens and also supports wallet services such as MyEtherWallet and MetaMask.

Uniswap is an open source network that allows the users to copy the code from the platform and build their own decentralized exchange. The centralized exchanges are more like intermediaries that are mainly driven by the profits unlike the DEXs. Another rare feature about the Uniswap platform is that users have complete control over their funds as against the centralized exchanges, which forces their traders to give up control. By doing so, the exchanges maintain complete control over their internal database, which can be easily manipulated and, on the other hand, it is an expensive and time consuming activity. All in all, Uniswap has over $3 billion worth of assets on its platform that is locked into their protocol. Since we have already understood the concept of the Uniswap platform, let us also understand how it works.

Process Behind Uniswap

Uniswap is powered by two types of smart contracts, namely, an exchange contract and a factory contract. We already know by now that smart contracts are functions that automatically take actions once certain conditions are met. The factory contract feature is used on the platform and facilitated is used to create a new exchange contract for any of the ERC-20 tokens or, in general, it is used to add new tokens to the platform. However, the exchange contract is usually used to trade all the tokens on the platform. The users can exchange any of their ERC-20 tokens with another through the Uniswap platform. Now that we know what type of protocol is used by Uniswap, let us take a look at their new trading model:

<u>Automated Liquidity Protocol</u>

Liquidity means that people in the market can easily buy or sell an asset without much of a price fluctuation. If there is low liquidity in the market, chances are that they will remain volatile, where high liquidity ensures price stability. Going back in time to 2017, cryptocurrencies were still opposed by masses, which meant that even a simple transaction in Bitcoin would cause a huge fluctuation in price. This was owing to the fact the crypto markets lacked liquidity, which made trading cryptocurrencies a costly activity.

Prior to Uniswap, most of the crypto trading would mainly take place through centralized exchanges such as Binance. So even though Bitcoin tried to influence decentralized transactions, trading in crypto tokens was still ruled by the traditional infrastructure that followed depositing funds under a single authority and trading through an orderbook system. When Uniswap was founded, it planned to solve one major problem in the market and that was eliminating the centralized exchanges. Let us take a look at how Uniswap solves the liquidity problems.

How Does Uniswap Provide Liquidity to Its Users?

The users on the Uniswap platform create a fund by pooling their money together, which is later used to execute all the trades on the platform. Every listed token on Uniswap has its own pool that is contributed by the users. The price of each token is settled upon using a math algorithm that is solved using the computer. We will take a short glimpse into how the price is determined in the next section.

Using the Automated Liquidity Protocol, the buyer or the seller does not have to necessarily wait for the other party to execute the order and complete the trade. This means instead of waiting for a while, users can immediately execute their trades at a known price quote as long as a particular pool has the liquidity to facilitate the orders.

Every time a user contributes the fund to the liquidity pool (LP), they receive a token which represents the stake that they have contributed to the pool. For instance, a user decides to contribute $20,000 to a liquidity pool that is holding a total asset value of $100,000. The user will get a token for contributing 20% of their funds to the liquidity pool. Now what should one do with this token? A user can collect these tokens and later redeem them for a share of their trading fee. Uniswap usually charges its users a flat fee of 0.30% for all the trades on Uniswap and they directly send this to the liquidity reserve on the platform.

Suppose a liquidity provider or the user has decided that they want to exit the pool, the user is eligible to receive some part of the total fees from this reserve depending upon their contribution to the pool. The proof of the stake that is owed to the user during the exit is recorded in the token. This will be wiped off when the user exits the liquidity pool. After understanding Uniswap's liquidity protocol, let us understand how the prices are determined on the Uniswap platform.

How Token Prices Are Determined on Uniswap?

The centralized exchange follows an order book system whereby every token price is determined using the highest bid price and the lowest ask price. (Bidders are usually buyers and sellers are the ones who ask for a price in exchange for their asset.) To automate the entire system, Uniswap decided to build an automated market maker formula. Through this system, Uniswap will adjust the price of each token through a mathematical equation based on demand and supply forces. This technique works effectively by increasing or decreasing the price of the token after considering the amount of coins supplied in each of the respective pools.

Let us try to understand this using a mathematical illustration and an example. For instance, the following equation is used to determine the price of every token on Uniswap:

$x*y=k$

Here, x will represent the value of token A and y will represent the value of token B. On the other hand, k will remain a constant whose value never changes. So, if a user wants to start trading chain-link (an ethereum token) for ether (ETH) token, they can use the LINK/ETH pool on the Uniswap platform. Now the user wants to clearly trade LINK tokens, so they add a large number of it to the pool, which, in turn, increases the ratio of LINK in the pool. Since the value of k will always remain constant, the price of LINK will decrease, whereas the price of ETH will increase. If the user keeps pumping the pool with LINK tokens, they will get less ETH tokens because its price has increased. (If you consider this from a demand and supply theory, the greater the supply, the lesser the price of the product; however, the greater the demand for the product, its price will rise.)

Lastly, the size of the liquidity pool is also an important factor that must be considered while determining the price of the token. The pool size mainly determines the price fluctuations of the tokens. For instance, the greater the money invested in a particular pool (which also means that the pool is highly liquid), the easier it will be for the users to make large trades in that pool without letting the price fall drastically.

Uniswap is a revolutionary decentralized application that has trumped various others in the race. Right from establishing a decentralized exchange to building a complete automated trading system, Uniswap has outperformed all the other DApps.

However, everything that you have seen until now was discovered either a decade ago or invented three years ago. Since then, things have changed. Today, there are many other DApps which are competing against their predecessors so that they can overtake them. Platforms like Tether and Quantstamp have been competing against MakerDAO trying to provide alternatives to people.

The technological transformation that we have seen today was just a dream three years ago. However, we have achieved it and this is just the beginning. All the developments that we have seen in the DeFi space today is like a beginner's programming course. Just like there will be more advanced level courses, there will also be various other applications in the DeFi ecosystem that will transform our financial system even further.

Why Defi Is Inevitable in the Future?

The DeFi ecosystem has the ability to help our system evolve for the better. It's outstanding characteristics is what makes it unique and different from all the other systems. However, there are many factors that are involved here which add up to make DeFi revolutionary. Let us take a look at some of these factors:

<u>Outperforms Obsolete System</u>

What makes DeFi different and desirable at the same time is the fact that it is autonomous. Imagine being in a place where you require permission to do everything, right from eating your breakfast to going for a bath. In the end, you will be frustrated and leave that place because it is controlling your every action. Our centralized system was trendy back in the day, but now they have become obsolete. We cannot possibly continue to work through a system where all our actions are controlled. DeFi gives the users their freedom to work independently within the system without having the need to identify other users. In short, the personal data remains secured while you still get to conduct transactions with users across the globe without having the need to seek any permission.

Powerful Process

The concept of decentralization is rather exceptional as it lets the system quit their dependency on a single factor whose downfall would potentially threaten their existence. For example, take a look at the banking system: Any problem within the central bank will cause a ripple effect across all the banks. Decentralization divides the power among the users, so even if one user falters, it won't necessarily affect another user.

Possibilities Beyond Imagination

Bitcoin was solely created for the purpose of transactions. However, later, the Ethereum blockchain was developed so that the users build protocols and create a financial system. There are so many decentralized apps and protocols today that offer you low-cost, high-speed financial services. Our system is evolving, our techniques are improving, and our technology is transforming. Going ahead, it is hard to even imagine the amount of growth that DeFi can contribute towards the future.

Bound to Happen

If you open your Twitter right now, you will see how the crypto community is talking about cryptos replacing fiat currency. This is the same Bitcoin that was rejected by public approval when it was first discovered. Now, everyone is slowly shifting towards the crypto assets and trying to own at least a few Bitcoin tokens. In the future, it is likely that DeFi will be adapted into our financial system and our lives. Since it is inevitable, why should we avoid it now anyway?

The financial revolution has already started to take its shape. In the near future, there will be a time when most of the underbanked society will finally be able to access financial services right from the touch of their smartphones. Let us take a look at some of the factors that highlight why DeFi is inevitable in the future:

- Three Indicators That Show DeFi Is Inevitable

- There are three major signs that DeFi will become a part of life at some point in the future.

  Some of these points are as follows:

- Tokens Are Revolutionizing DeFi

NFTs weren't even invented back in the day. Imagine suddenly getting a thought one day where you can create a token of your artwork and sell it to make money. As crazy as it sounds, it is happening as tokens are truly revolutionizing the entire DeFi ecosystem. In fact, there are more and more people who are coming forward to create an NFT for their creative work so that they can sell it online.

ICOs Will Replace IPOs

Until now, Wall Street only awaited the arrival of a new Initial Public Offering (IPO) in the market because they believed that the stock would outperform the market. Now there are Initial Coin Offerings (ICOs), mainly for the purpose of listing new crypto coins of centralized exchanges. Many people have already shifted their assets from stocks to crypto tokens. It is indicative of the fact that ICOs will be the next new trend and IPOs will soon run out of steam.

Deteriorating Banking Infrastructure

Our banking structures were flawed since the day they were discovered. Sometimes a user might feel safe conducting their banking activity under the centralized infrastructure, but it is nothing more than a facade. The banking infrastructure will collapse and turn to dust some day. A few years ago, it would have been a distant dream. Here are some of the reasons why the people are begging for a new system to take roots and fly high:

People want control. Whether it is through a bank or by themselves, people want their control on everything, especially money.

Exchange without any concern. Transferring money without having to deal with the hassle of the authorities is another reason why people want DeFi to be introduced into their system.

Everybody wants freedom. Some want it from their lives and others from their career. However, all the Bitcoin lovers here only want the current financial system to become free from the shackles of centralized authority.

Looking at all the above factors simultaneously, it is understood that DeFi will revolutionize our future in the coming days. The DeFi revolution had already begun a long time ago. The only question that remains unanswered is, "Are you ready for it?"

Conclusion

Decentralized Finance, also known as DeFi systems, is a revolutionary concept as we know it and it is about to change the face of the global financial system. By now, we know that DeFi has capabilities beyond what the human brain can truly comprehend. With DeFi getting implemented in the future, things will truly change. The financial framework will be autonomous. Users will connect directly to borrow loans or deposit money. The way our financial system has been functioning until today will crumble and a new era will begin. What we can do is just embrace this new change that will truly be an evolution for us as human beings.

Most of the time, people are finding it hard to believe that Bitcoin could ever be adapted as a currency. However, if you look at the way things are changing rapidly in the DeFi ecosystem, it is obvious that DeFi is about to change the roadmap of the financial systems in the future and there is no way anyone can stop it. After all, in the decade of technological evolution, if we are still stuck going to the banks, we have truly not evolved.

As readers, what you can simply do is read and educate yourself. The only true way to gain financial freedom is by empowering yourself and becoming financially literate. Three years ago, there was no such concept like NFT. Whatever has been discovered today is mainly led by the fact that people are becoming more financially literate as they try to evolve with the system. That is the only way we can truly become knowledgeable about the new developments in this space.

Now that you have read the entire book, here are some of the key things that you must remember at all times:

DeFi is a decentralized financial system that brings autonomy into the picture, allowing users to interact with each other without having the need for intermediaries. Most of the DeFi ecosystem is powered by smart contracts that will carry out actions based on a given set of instructions. Lastly, every transaction on DeFi is recorded into the distributed ledger, which allows you to view the transaction history without any hesitation.

Bitcoin may have been the original crypto but Ethereum definitely stole the show with its unique blockchain technology that has the ability to let DApps be drawn over it. Protocols like Compound and Uniswap are truly transformational and offer great services to their users. These protocols have truly transformed the entire financial system.

There are so many benefits for getting into the DeFi system. The number one benefit is that you are in charge of your own money, which means you don't have to depend on others or even worry about financial losses. Another is that it has fastened the process, so no more waiting in the line for that loan verification, which would anyway charge you a higher interest rate.

Lastly, DeFi is about to take over the entire world economy at some point where everyone works on their own and is in charge of their own funding. Such decentralization will not only help you to gain access to the world's most revolutionary technology but also be the master of your own universe.

Lastly, before I end this book, I just want to thank all my readers for picking this up and letting it guide you through the DeFi journey. It was never an easy one to begin with, but by the end of this book, I am sure that all of you have learned great lessons from understanding basic concepts to realizing the importance of DeFi. The fact that this book is in your hand right now is the key that you truly believe in this system and wish to learn more about it.

During the beginning days of my DeFi journey, I too was unaware, just like you. Today, I have been able to learn enough to put all the wisdom into these pages. Through this book, I wish to feel empowered enough to make the right financial decisions. With the help of this book, I am hoping that you have learnt tons of new lessons. Now that you are aware that the future of global finance mainly lies with DeFi taking over the world, what are you waiting for? Get started with those crypto investments today.